SYMMETRICAL EDUCATION

SYMMETRICAL EDUCATION

OR

THE IMPORTANCE OF JUST PROPORTION

IN MIND AND BODY

BY

W. CAVE THOMAS

'This is an art
Which does mend nature,—change it rather;
But the art itself is nature'
WINTER'S TALE

LONDON
SMITH, ELDER, & CO., 15 WATERLOO PLACE
1873

PREFACE.

—◆◆—

IT HAS often been remarked that the present intellectual tendency is to level all the old ramparts—formal restrictions as they are called—in politics, education, literature, and art—not, as the writer believes, from any wanton and destructive spirit, but because the nature of the errors, the extremes they were intended to guard against, and the whole substratum of theory on which they were raised, have long since been forgotten. The old school forgets that the public mind has been brought more and more into contact with scientific enquiry during the last half century, and hence has gradually acquired a taste for exact demonstration, and for probing to first principles. It therefore distrusts those dicta and generalizations which are dogmatically tendered for its guidance. It desires to know more about their foundations before consenting to be led by, or coerced to observe them.

The principles of morality, education and art now in vogue are for the most part dogmatical ; we know not the how, the when, or the where, they were obtained. Nor ought the few who by education or an intuitive feeling think and act in conformity with the old-fashioned rules and teaching, to complain of the revolt, seeing how few there are of their own school who can give the reasons for the faith that is in them. This modern irreverent seeming towards ancient formula does not proceed from any permanently rebellious or dangerous disposition, but rather from a praiseworthy desire to find some surer scientific basis for thought and action than the teachers of the old régime are disposed to afford. It should be recollected that our æsthetic education has for centuries been based upon pagan models, and that the contempt for the ancient forms of literature and art which has of late grown up in England and America is only one of the many manifestations of a wide-spread iconoclastic undiscriminating dissent—of the rude virtue of protesting—which will some day be moderated and moulded to grand results. The aborigines of a new world of ideas, as of a newly discovered country, are inevitably barbarous; they refuse to submit to the restraints and hamper of fashion, prefer their own primitive nakedness, and to readjust and build up their principles anew, and for themselves—wattle and mud though their wigwams may be. Such a state of things may shock, does shock, the classically cultivated intellect; nevertheless there is much in all this rude vigour to console the earnest thinker, viz., that there is a desire to seek the true foundations on which to rebuild. A great poet once observed to some coxcomb who was bemoaning the 'small Latin, and still less Greek,' of Shakespere: 'Sir! the more to his honour, he went to the well-head. We may rather consider ourselves fortunate that his great intellect was never fettered by classical learning.' And this admonition from a poet to a poetaster ought to be taken to heart by Snobdom, for we are great only where we have built upon independent foundations—for ourselves, instead of upon precedent.

Now the theory that quantity is the fundamental form of phenomena, relativity, experience, is the ultimate form of cognition, appears to afford that enduring, immutable basis on which to reconstruct our principles, re-establish science; for the quantitative theory leads to exact, definite statements in all branches of enquiry; the setting forth of principles in those forms in which the greatest exactitude of expression is possible, measure and number. And not only are the advantages of the quantitative theory not confined to the means which it affords for exact enunciation, but it enables us to detect common principles obtaining in every department of investigation, laws which alike rule in the planetary system and human nature—laws of just proportional relation which hold equally good in ethics, politics, education, æsthetics, physics, &c.

We should, nevertheless, note that this 'barbarous,' 'irreverent,' 'iconoclastic' crowd, however prone it may be to reject ancient dogma it cannot fathom, still looks forward with a reserved reverence towards an ideal manhood. Now the constitution of this regal or ideal humanity, which these destructives, as they are called, indistinctly perceive enthroned, is that which has to be clearly defined, and which the education of the future has to develope. The quantitative theory enables us to define this ideal humanity. But it would be useless either to talk about its definition or development, unless human nature were plastic and capable of being materially *modified, remoulded, reformed, rectified* intellectually and physically. I shall, therefore, endeavour to show in the following chapters how human, like other organic nature, is capable of being gradually developed to a purpose, that purpose being its symmetrical or proportionate reconstitution. How both the intellectual and physical natures may be deteriorated and deformed by neglect and injudicious training, or rectified and symmetrically proportioned by a right system of education.

Do not imagine that, in writing of a prevalent irreverence towards old forms, restrictions, or conventions, I myself believe them all to be wrong. I believe, on the contrary, that many of them are perfectly right, and that the world will in due course be of that opinion too ; but there is a very great difference between receiving with an unquestioning obedience, working upon dead formal precedents, and working with living, self-earned principles, derived from an independent and careful study of nature. In disparaging as it may have seemed classical and venerable precedents, I have only conformed my expressions to the general *pose* of modern thought—I have also endeavoured to show that this has a good apology to offer for its somewhat defiant, rough and ungraceful attitude.

The great impediments in the way of, and which prevent the realisation of ideal human nature, the regal manhood, are the false notions prevalent in respect to the true aim of education; or if not in respect to the true object—as that is perhaps generally understood to be intellectual power—at least as to the proper means of obtaining this power. The two most prevalent and formidable vulgar errors on the subject are—that intellectual capacity is in proportion to the *quantity* of information acquired; and that the natural bias or idiosyncrasy, either of the individual intellect or physique, should be cultivated; the latter error leading to a still further exaggeration of bias, *i.e.* of disproportion; whereas we hope to prove that the 'regality' of which we have spoken inheres in the perfectly proportioned, balanced or symmetrical humanity. We must, therefore, escape from these misleadings as soon as possible. More especially should we now be on our guard against the fatal and prevalent preference for *quantity* instead of *quality* in education, when our middle classes and workmen are crying out, the one for advanced, the other for technical education—'More subjects! more subjects of instruction!' Why, this is indicative, not of *advanced* but retrograde views on the subject. The advanced education, the education of the future, will commence when people shall begin to perceive that intellectual power will be greatest when the mind is trained, developed as an intellectual instrument, and that 'cramming,' and study of more than the essential subjects adds nothing to capacity; but, in fact, that such a practice weakens the intellectual power in the ratio in which it is pushed to extreme. Greece and Rome furnish abundant evidence that humanity was intellectually as great, nay greater, in art, literature, politics, and arms, without our modern and vast acquisitions of physical knowledge; and, therefore, that these are not essential to the development of the full capacity of the human intellect. If we desire to be a free, a great people, we must no longer cry out for a more and more extended curriculum of acquirements, for *quantity*, but for symmetrical education, for greater simplicity and *quality*. If the country persists in its present misleading and wrong-headedness in respect to education, it will do nothing well, and rapidly retrograde.

The present essay may suffer in some degree in

being detached from a more extensive work.* The reader will readily discover that some of my material has been appropriated, and that my merit, if merit it be, is in having marshalled and recombined facts according to principles of the highest order of generality, the Quantitative Theory.

W. C. T.

* The Immutable Mean, or the Quantitative Principles of the Kosmos, applied to Ethics, Politics, Education, Art, and Natural Theology. All Phenomena quantifiable, all Relativity fundamentally proportional.

CONTENTS.

CHAPTER I.

ADDENDA.

SYMMETRICAL EDUCATION.

CHAPTER I.

GENERAL ARGUMENT IN FAVOUR OF A PROPORTIONATE OR SYM-
METRICAL DEVELOPMENT, AND AGAINST THE COMMON PRACTICE
OF CULTIVATING INDIVIDUAL BIAS, I.E. DISPROPORTION.—THE
VULGAR ERROR REFUTED THAT INTELLECTUAL POWER IS IN
PROPORTION TO THE NUMBER OF SUBJECTS ACQUIRED, OR
THAT QUANTITY IS OF GREATER IMPORTANCE THAN QUALITY.

THE SUBJECT of Education is one which claims our
most earnest and prompt consideration, for by its
means is mankind to attain to that *vita nuova*, or
new life, in the world which is alike a prevision of
prophecy and science.

The principle of our present system of education,
if it really have any principle dominating it, is that of
developing the strongest *natural bias*. At the first
blush, the notion seems to have a common-sense
reasonableness, but it is nevertheless erroneous, and
practically fraught with mischief. It misleads parents
and teachers, and prevents the public from discern-
ing the true and legitimate aim of educational

B

culture. Our teachers, ignorant of the law of symmetry, and of the measure of rectitude expressed by the golden mean, endeavour to isolate and inordinately develop special faculties. This cannot be done, as we shall presently show, but at the expense of, or by the still further deterioration of others, but by increasing the original congenital disproportion, the original amount of aberration from an ideal standard. The procedure is alike inimical to the development of common sense, unanimity, and beauty, and mental and physical deformity are the inevitable results of the system. It is this, the modern system of education, which keeps society unbalanced, which promotes biassed, one-sided opinion, fanaticism, and madness.

In this country we fail in two very important particulars—pure theory and pure taste; and the corrective for both, we believe, will be found in that more scientific and rational system of education which insists on the proportionate or symmetrical development of all the human faculties; *for as men become more symmetrically and perfectly developed are their views enlarged, are their affections and tastes purified. The mastery is to him who is moderate, attempered, and balanced in his entire nature.**

The present system, however, instead of aiming at this rounded, symmetrical, and balanced nature, pets and encourages the congenital bias, or the acciden-

* 'He that striveth for the mastery is temperate in all things.'— I *Cor.* ix. 25.

tally acquired predilections of a child, in apparently total ignorance of a very well-ascertained fact, that any abnormal exhibition of strength in one direction must inevitably be accompanied with some special weakness in another. This is what is called, in common parlance, strengthening and developing natural genius and character, and is as consistent as it would be to promote a tendency to obesity or to vice; it is indeed, in a certain sense, increasing a vicious excess, a morbid extension of an already morbid tendency. It is a wrong leading which should be immediately checked, and henceforth a greater care given to the cultivation of those qualities which tend to balance or neutralise the erratic individuality. In cases of more obvious disproportion, the skilful physician endeavours to strengthen the weaker and less-developed portion of the human frame. It is not the strong limb that requires his art; nor do over-endowed mental faculties need the same attention or educational skill as the weaker; the stronger will always be self-helpful. The true policy of education is to establish, by every means in its power, a balance between the dominant and weaker states of accidental organization. The opposite course tends to biassed opinions, and to separate and isolate various branches of study; to prevent large views of science and art; to make professors and students magnify their speciality, and study it as the all in all apart, and not in reference to the whole together. Instead of the ideal man, we have extraordinary individuality of character; instead of science, disconnected fragmentary observation and study; without the bond of life. We have to choose then between two distinct systems of education, the individuating and the symmetrical, *i.e.* the disproportioning and proportioning; between that advocating the development of individual predeliction or bias, and that whose object is to check individual bias or excess by advancing faculties in defect. The latter is that in conformity with the great law of symmetry we have derived from the study of the Cosmos. The more comprehensive our study of nature, the clearer do we perceive that equalisation or balance is the goal of progress. But there are not wanting partisans of an opposite doctrine to declare that such a condition of things, if attainable, would be undesirable. But look to the teachings of history. Has not man, in spite of all impediments of opposition and difficulties, attained to a more equable distribution of means and powers? Nevertheless, the opponents of equable or symmetrical development assert that it is as vain to attempt to make men equal as to make two watches go precisely alike. But, difficult as this may practically be, it is yet the end to be desired and striven for by the watchmaker. The analogy, so far from controverting, materially strengthens and illustrates our argument;

for the first imperfect timepieces varied considerably more than the chronometers of the present day. What is progress in this case but an advance towards equality of character, perfection? and if it be the object of ethics to convert and conform men to an *ideal standard*, mental and physical resemblance must inevitably increase as humanity approaches, is moulded to such a standard. If your ethical and educational systems present you with an ideal it is impossible to approach, much less realise, depend upon it they are worthless. We all know, from our own observation of men trained in certain public schools, that they are unified by being subjected to a common influence and discipline; that they are thus assimilated in tastes, modes of thought, and general bearing, and banded together through life for mutual admiration and support.

The lower we descend in the scale of being, the more limited, the more technical—if it may so be expressed—the purpose of a species; the more marked its individuality, its characteristic—the more extreme its proportions. In contemplating the structure of animals, we cannot fail to be struck with their wonderful *special* adaptation to some special purpose. It is this correlation between structure and purpose which enables the anatomist to interpret the fossil records of a former condition of the earth, and to write the history of extinct species. There are, doubtless, many creatures at the confines of—at that point where the characteristic of one species merges into that of another—the neutral point, the habits of which it would be more difficult to determine. It is perhaps the mixed nature of man which puzzles investigators, which forms the enigma so difficult to solve ; for certain it is, that the relation between his organisation and capacity is not in general clearly discerned, or it may be that the individualities and minute variations by which man distinguishes his fellow-men, preclude the attainment of that distant point of view which renders the minute differences of other species of being indistinct, and which resolves them into their general characteristics. It has been observed by a talented author, that from such a point of view the fundamental resemblance which lurks below various appearances is often startling.

The tendency to average is perhaps a mental necessity of a moderated and equable nature. That a being so constituted should average is at least consistent ; and if the tendency to a balanced organisation be the goal towards which man is tending, we should expect to find this characteristic reflected in those operations by which he reconciles the external world to himself; and such is the case. To diminish extreme distances, to level mountains, to straighten the course of rivers, to counteract the extremities of wind and wave, and equalise the irregularities of temperature, are only a few of the instances in which he manifests a natural tendency to surround himself with mean or average conditions; in this light, perhaps, his true purpose and character appear as moderator and lord of the earth.

In a former work it was demonstrated that there are only two possible tendencies in relativity, viz. to parity and disparity. We have then to discover which is the *ascending*, which the descending, scale of being.

Now if the structure of animals, birds, reptiles, &c., be considered in their combinations of bones, muscles, and nerves, they will be found to possess a greater *disparity* of power than man; that is to say, in the former particular powers are advanced at the expense of others for special purposes. Nature holds, as it were, a scale of opposite advantages: when she bestows a preponderance on one side, it is in the ratio of that subtracted from the other; if she confers some favours too liberally, she at the same time denies others. In man alone does she endeavour to mete them equally.

The variations between the relative organic developments of different powers in the same being lie between their maximum and minimum extremes; and our object will be to show that human organisation, at its best, is an aggregation of moderate faculties, of faculties developed midway between their possible extremes; and that this aggregate of moderate organisation, paradoxical as it may appear, represents the maximum of general and brain power. No one can contemplate a natural history collection without being struck with numerous instances of creatures strangely formed; but if to this first impression the history of the habits of each be called to mind, and compared with its structure, it overcomes even that natural repugnance to forms of being widely differing from us.

The lower orders of creation are confined to one routine; the history of a day is the history of a life—like human mechanical inventions, destined to fulfil one special purpose and no other. Whereas man, superadded to his daily wants, has a mental nature capable of improvement. It is not to-day as it was in ages past; its history is yet incomplete and purpose unfulfilled, ever expanding with fresh experience to encompass the sphere of the knowable. In this tendency to sphericity is involved that to equality of power in all directions, contra-distinguishing him from creatures of mere instinct, which continually move in one plane. Hence we see that to technicalize man into any special groove is to adopt the descending scale.

What disparity in the organisation of other animated creatures compared with man whose representative elements may be found some in one, some in another, extended and exaggerated in particular directions, showing that *in the ratio that any special function is urged to an extreme, is it accompanied with some special inferiority, or defect, and a loss of general power !*

' In a comparison of the frame and capabilities of man with those of the inferior animals, if we take the human frame as the ideal standard of form, it will be found that all others present so many declensions from the idea, by *exaggeration* or *defect*; and it will be found from this survey that man is unquestionably endowed with that structure the perfection of which is revealed in such a balanced relation of the parts to a whole as may best fit it for a being exercising intelligent choice, and destined for moral freedom. It is not, therefore, an absolute perfection of the constituents singly, but the proportional development of all, and their harmonious constitution to one, for which we contend: a constitution which implies in a far higher degree than in any other animal a balanced relation of the living powers and faculties, and which requires, therefore, in man pre-eminently the endowment of rational will as necessary for the control and adjustment of the balance.

* * * * *

' Hence the departure from the perfect proportion of man, which we observe in the inferior animals, may be regarded as deformities of *exaggeration* or *defect*, dependent upon a preponderance of a part that necessitates a particular use, or the absence of a part that deprives the animal of a power, and in both instances alike abrogates that freedom for which provision is made in the balanced relation of the constituents of the human fabric which permits the free choice of means, and the adaptation to any purpose determined by an intelligent free-will.   Dilate the head, and we have a symptom of disease ; protrude the jaws, you have a voracious animal ; lengthen the ears, timidity is expressed ; let the nose project, and the animal is governed by its scent ; enlarge the belly, and you are reminded of the animal appetites ; long arms may fit him for an inhabitant of the trees, and make him a fit companion for the ape, and predominant length of legs is infallibly associated with the habits of the wading or leaping animals.   In all regarding man's form with reference to his destination as the ideal standard, the means become ends, deformity prevails, and becomes the badge of unintelligent slavery to the mere animal nature.'

As there is an obvious analogy between the human form and that of an ordinary mammalian quadruped, by comparing sections of the structure of the former with their representatives in the latter, the characteristics of special and general adaptation will be at once illustrated.

The Head.—The facial section of animals is more protuberant and excessive compared with that receptive of the brain ; the jaws longer, the immediate organisation of the senses larger. In man the facial angle is raised towards the mean or point of angular indifference between the acute and obtuse; the senses are retracted and more equal in their divisions. The Greeks discovered this tendency, and realised it in their ideal sculpture. The nervous organisation of the eye, ear, and nose, by this retraction, are brought into more central cerebral relations; his senses are less independently perceptive than in animals. The first impressions of seeing, hearing, and smelling in the latter are more acute, more instinctive; those of man require the corrections of experience and judgment; their proximity to a nervous centre excites comparison and reason, and thus a *special* inferiority is counterbalanced by increased cerebral capacity. It is this very deficiency of intuition in man which constitutes his greatness; if it had been otherwise, he would have had no incitement either to acquire knowledge, preserve, or communicate it. But if some of the senses are more acute in animals, others are less so. The *inequality* between the organs of seeing, hearing, and smelling becomes greater as they descend in the scale. Even in the mammalia this disparity is very evident, sometimes in an over-adequacy for general but not particular purposes, at others below the centre of the scale of power, as not being required. In the feline race the eye is adapted for vision in a subdued light; the glare of day is consequently irritating and painful to them ; their scent is also keen ; both of which suit them for prowling and predatory habits. But if the organs of vision are dominant and peculiarly extended in one line of direction in the carnivora, those of hearing and seeing have also extreme and peculiar modifications ; in the herbivorous tribes, as the ferocious are led by scent, the timid are warned by the ear ; the sight of the former is fitted for night, that of the latter for extended vision by day. Thus, in the order of things a balance of chances between escape and destruction is instituted.

The Neck and Trunk.—The cervical vertebræ are found to be extra-developed lengthwise in the giraffe, camel, stag, horse, &c. ; whereas in the hog, elephant, hippopotamus, and others, these are extremely retracted ; the number is the same, but longer or shorter in proportion to man. The trunk, too, in quadrupeds occupies a larger proportion of the whole frame than in the human subject.

The Limbs. — The metacarpal and metatarsal bones are lengthened into stilts for swiftness in the digitigrade, as in the horse, deer, and many other quadrupeds ; while in the plantigrade, such as the bear, sloth, &c., the bones and the phalanges become extremely developed as paws. The range of movement of the limbs of both these divisions is chiefly confined to one plane, whereas those of man are more capable of movement in every direction ; his arm can move through the greater portion of a sphere; even his lower limbs, which are naturally more confined, have much greater power of rotation than the corresponding members in the former, and by exercise these may attain a range almost as extensive as that of the arms. The disposition of his muscles, also, is more even than in quadrupeds; the bones of which are sometimes almost denuded, at others thickly enveloped.

But if the mammalian quadrupeds exhibit *disparity* of organisation when compared with man, how much more do those still lower in the scale! But as the fact was strongly confirmed by that comparison, instead of with these, it lends additional force to the argument. It is hoped, however, that that which has been made will have sufficiently confirmed the position previously assumed—that man's pre-eminence in the scale of being is physiologically dependent on a greater *equality* in the subdivisions of his frame, in the power of moving his limbs in different directions, and in the less susceptibility of his senses. His head was found to be more equally divided between the face and the cavity of the brain; the joints of his limbs *central*, and in his variations of proportion approximating *mean* rather than extreme differences; his limbs possessing, though less extended in their motion in some one particular direction, a moderate degree of movement through the larger portion of a sphere.

In the constitution of his senses, if his eye be not so far-sighted as the eagle, his scent not so keen as the lion, nor hearing as sensitive as that of the hare, neither is he deficient in these qualities, but has them equally developed in a *mean* proportional degree. The more nature is interrogated, the more imperatively does it point to equable or balanced organisation as the ideal of the highest type ; consequently the further man departs from this standard, the nearer does he approach the characteristic individuality of the brute—*disparity* of powers—and it is very remarkable, or it might be said a natural consequence, that inordinate or excessive organisation in human nature in special directions does produce a certain affinity or resemblance in its outward form to those animals which have the same peculiarities in still greater excess.

We have, therefore, by an inductive process, confirmed that more general conclusion at which we arrived by our quantitative analysis of phenomena, viz. that nature must either tend to parity or disparity, and that the former is the progressive, formative, and constructive tendency, the latter the retrogressive, deformative, and destructive.

Man, therefore, rises in the scale of nature as he approaches that constitution which we have described as a concentration of moderate faculties, and descends as he becomes excentrated from this, the symmetrical organization. The positions may be thus stated :—

1. Beings in which the greatest number of faculties are concentrated in their *mean* degree of development manifest the largest *general* power.

2. Beings in which any special faculty is excessively developed manifest *special* aptitudes, but exhibit deficiency in general power in proportion to the excentration which constitutes their characteristic.

It is very commonly, but erroneously, conceived that 'concentration' consists in a man devoting himself exclusively to one particular pursuit, and ignoring all others, when in reality this is *ex*centration, a partial or isolated application which is sure to lead to biassed and incomplete views. True, 'concentration' consists in bringing all kinds of knowledge to bear upon a special pursuit, which is then, not only thoroughly understood in itself, but in its relation to the whole together. You may observe by the demeanour of the students of any special branch of inquiry that they believe themselves to be the observed of all observers, the neophytes of the only science or art worthy of public consideration. Such a feeling would not exist if education were founded upon a higher philosophy which points to the enchainment and correlation of phenomena.

So far the argument leads to the general conclusion that the ascending tendency of being, as observed in nature, is to a concentration of faculties in their *mean* degree, and points the direction in which education should exert its powers in order to exercise its most beneficent influence on the destiny of man. It was natural that men, emerging from barbarism, should regard the antique world with extreme veneration, and believe everything they mentally required was to be derived from studying classical literature and art. But now that the day of free and independent inquiry has dawned, we may fearlessly interrogate nature, with reference to a more efficient and practical system of training than that established in the middle ages, when there was no freedom of opinion.

Leaving these more general observations, we will take up the thread of the all-embracing Quantitative Theory, according to which all things exist in definite proportions, of the theory which demonstrates that there is a mid or *mean* degree in the possible fluctuation of any species of phenomenon which has been recognised by different minds, and in different branches of inquiry, as the common measure of perfection and rectitude, in morals, art, science, &c. The principle of moderation is the most ancient scientific generalisation we possess, has the testimony of a greater length of experience than, perhaps, any other truth. If the mean then be the common measure of both the moral and physical ideals, education, as a formative art, has to extirpate disproportion, and realize those ideals. Now this could only be accomplished on one condition, namely, the plasticity of human nature or its capability of being modified by the transfer of superabundant vitality from one portion of the system to another less endowed, and which needs greater activity, and so by undoing excess making good defect. We have now to show that human nature is plastic, and modifiable ; other-wise, all suggestions for its rectification, its *re*-forma-tion, would be in vain.

CHAPTER II.

THE MODIFIABILITY OF HUMAN NATURE RENDERS ITS SYMMETRICAL DEVELOPMENT OR RECTIFICATION POSSIBLE.

WHATEVER value we may set upon the ultimate conclusions of the recent works on the origin of species, of man, one great fact is revealed in those inquiries, viz., that life forms are exceedingly plastic and modifiable, and that great transformations have occurred within known periods of time, either by a fortuitous concourse of external circumstances, or by design. Man has learnt by experience how to develop special forms of animal and vegetable life, to conform them to his requirements; and had he devoted as much attention to the improvement of human organisation and form, we should have doubtless, long ere this, witnessed its beneficial results, for they are no less plastic and modifiable.

From the earliest condition of the living being to its end, it would appear constantly decreasing in modifiability, infancy and age being the extremes of the scale; the first half of life being that in which it may be most dominated by, and the latter that in which it most dominates, external conditions. Animals, for the most part, attain full development in a brief period, and are independent sooner after birth; whereas man, at his first coming into the world, is feeble, helpless, and entirely devoid of knowledge; he therefore needs strength, assistance, and judgment. Even his senses are not then developed, but supposing they were, he could make no use of them, not having as yet compared his sensations, much less distinguished them; he perceives no external objects; in a word, he is an almost insensible automaton, and a scarcely animated statue. The senses gradually unfold : by degrees an infant learns to see and feel, the faculties of the mind afterwards expand with those of the body, and both are fully developed by exercise. The length of time which man requires to attain maturity ought to be esteemed a special privilege conferred by a beneficent Creator for some great end. Animals are sooner adapted to their limited conditions of being ; but man, as Wisdom's minister on earth, is granted this long state of probation that the Divine laws may be instilled while his organisation is in that plastic condition most fitted to receive a deep impression of them, and to be moulded to its right forms and uses. This privilege, however, is not sufficiently valued, and therefore not converted to its best uses ; instead of a rational domination of the pliant period of youth, there is a lifeless routine miscalled education.

External forces, as we have said, dominate organisation in the earlier stages of being. It is not till the acorn has become a stately tree that it bids defiance to the blast and affords shelter under its branches. The germ may fall on stony ground and rot ; take root and struggle for existence in a crevice far too narrow for its mature demands; competing in soil already thickly preoccupied for light and air, run up a weak lank stem ; or, continuing the catalogue of adverse causes, either springing from under some super-imposed weight, or from being exposed to winds from one quarter, become either stunted or warped. Man is no less subject to analogous vicissitudes in the first periods of his existence. During the dependent and impressible ages of childhood and youth, he is oftener the sport of unfavourable circumstances, of which his maturity is the confirmed jest ; but as he approaches the adult state, he begins more and more to dominate the outward world, and as it may have meted to him, he metes to it again : if it has been favourable to intellectual growth, he employs himself either in suggesting or advancing schemes for social improve-ment, or in adding to our material advantages, by subjugating sea, river, rock, the elements, and even the subtle electricity to useful ends ; if adverse he undermines the foundations of society, scoffs at order, and suddenly darkens the world with atrocities and crimes. With these facts before us, what a responsi-bility is attached to education ! Education lays the foundations of society, and as these are either stable or unstable will the whole political and social fabric be enduring or transitory? In the vegetable kingdom the effects of unfavourable external conditions are very striking: if plants be transferred to an inferior soil and neglected, they gradually degenerate, all their former qualities declining, till they reach that point of retrenchment in organisation adapted to their altered and poorer circumstances. In animals a similar effect is produced by scanty sustenance and removal from the watchful care of man. Look, for instance, at the diminutive race of cattle feeding on the scanty herbage of the desolate moors of the North, or again at those diseased by his cruelty or folly, stimulated to their utmost powers, now strained with tottering limbs, now fattened into helplessness. There are conditions of deficiency and excess in food and use which are alike prejudicial to beings by diverting organisation from *that perfect central condition in which well-being consists.* Nor is man exempted by the all-wise Ruler from the penalties attached to the infringement of this great law. It is no mere analogy; the same relative conditions produce the same relative effects in him as in those beings lower in the scale of creation, as may be daily witnessed around us.

About two hundred years ago a number of people were driven by a barbarous policy from the counties of Antrim and Down, in Ireland, towards the sea coast, where they have ever since been settled, but in unusually miserable circumstances, even for Ireland, and the consequence is they exhibit peculiar features of the most repulsive kind, projecting jaws, with large open mouths, depressed noses, high cheek bones, and bow legs, together with an extremely diminutive stature. These, with an abnormal slenderness of the limbs, are the outward marks of a low and barbarous condition all over the world ; it is particularly seen in the Australian aborigines. 'Coarse, unwholesome, and ill-prepared food,' says Buffon, 'makes the human race degenerate ; all those people who live miserably are ugly and ill made.' Mental degeneracy, too, is its accompaniment ; those powers which rightly directed constitute the dignity of man, fall away, and instead of bequeathing a noble history to posterity, encumbers it with chronicles of crime ; without the compass of reason man is left a wreck in a sea of passion. Look at the criminal statistics, and for the tens who dishonour education, there are thousands who claim the pity due to ignorance and poverty. We know we are only reiterating but feebly what others have, and are now crying aloud ; we only contribute to the gradually gathering utterances, which must ultimately thunder an irresistible appeal for a more extended and enlightened system of education.

How numerous are the deformities occasioned by unfavourable circumstances in organisation ! Look at that terrible form of humanity, cretinism, the causes of which have been discovered to be atmospheric and other peculiar conditions of the valleys in mountainous districts—in short, endemic—this is a marked instance; or, again, at those produced by certain one-sided mental and physical occupations which cripple mind and body. Having briefly scanned those conditions which depress, we proceed to the consideration of such as have an opposite tendency, or to elevate organisation; for *in the knowledge of those causes which either increase or decrease the faculties, lies the power of education to modify or mould human nature towards its ideal, measured or moral form.*

Infinitely more scientific attention has been bestowed on the development of vegetable and animal structures than that of man; especially of those which are more immediately necessary or useful. In agriculture, for instance, the largest yield of grain from the smallest space being the desideratum, stimulated scientific men to seek those external conditions most conducive to the result required, and it is well known how successfully this research has been prosecuted. Over those animals, too, which have been domesticated for various purposes, what dominion has not experience given, enabling man not only to produce a general development of this or that particular species, but also a particular organisation of the species? As in the horse for strength, general purposes, or swiftness. In the ox, the long horned, short horned, white faced, &c. In sheep, the short legged, long legged, black faced, &c. The agriculturist and the breeder of cattle know by experience that such and such given conditions produce certain results, and thus, though perhaps unconsciously, tend to confirm the proposition *that organisation may be controlled to a purpose.* If we turn to the consideration of man, instances are of easy enumeration which clearly show to what extent organisation may be urged, and that any particular manifestation may be more or less induced by exercise proportionately to the favourable or unfavourable predisposition of innate structural condition. In various mechanical pursuits what dexterity is gained by constant practice; in performing on musical instruments, what rapid and complex movements of the fingers; in professional dancers and athletes, what strength and flexibility of limb; in the prize-fighters, what muscular development; in the blind, what an abnormal sense of touch! Yet all these result from continued voluntary or necessitated exercise. It is no less the case with the mental faculties; it is ever exercise which develops and strengthens.

Of what little service are congenital compared with acquired powers, even in those whose talents are attributed to great natural genius. Let the mathematician, with his logical subtlety of discrimination, compare his present powers with those he had at fourteen, or the great artist his ability of delineating forms with that possessed at the same age. What were Sir Isaac Newton and Michael Angelo at this period of their career? What was the amount of their innate compared with their achieved greatness?

When treating of the conditions which debase organisation, we alluded to the discovery that the atmospherical and other phenomena peculiar to the valleys of mountainous districts were the causes of cretinism; an establishment was therefore founded beyond such influences, to which those afflicted were removed as early as possible. The results were most favourable, and in this extreme case it has been proved that the controlling and compelling of organisation towards a higher type is not, as it was deemed, hopeless—science in this, as in other cases, subjugating evil.

All the preceding instances, we think, incontestably show that a *second* nature may be superinduced on the original stock. This will, perhaps, readily meet with an assent; it is often assented to in the familiar adage, 'Use is second nature;' but like many other isolated inductive generalisations, which have accumulated in the storehouse of experience, its full importance is but slowly recognised. We desire to see man's *second* nature developed under the guidance of reason.

How hopeful is the doctrine of acquired, compared with the fatal one of innate talent. Let those who are weak believe they may become stronger ; let every one doubt the efficacy of inherent genius, for they who remain passive, in the full confidence of possessing it, may live to hear the achieved talent of others acknowledged and their own disallowed.

Without cultivation he who has received from nature the most perfect, has no advantage over him who has received an inferior organisation ; but supposing them to be animated by an equal energy of application to study, their efforts would be attended with very different results. Whilst the former would surmount without difficulty the greatest obstacles, and advance with a rapid flight towards truth, easily penetrating the relations of phenomena, the attempts of the latter would be obstructed by natural impediments, and his progress slower towards the goal. But those who have received from nature a high degree of organic sensibility, and those who are inferiorly endowed, seldom possess an equal tendency to cultivate it ; those having acute natural perceptions have not the same urgent motives to application as they who are inferior in this respect ; the former is apt to lull into inactivity, while the latter stimulates to improvement, so that nature itself implants a motive to second the exertions of the educator who judiciously takes advantage of the modifiability of human nature. It is, therefore, something more than hypothetical, that just as debased organisation, from various causes, may be promoted and perpetuated in our species, perfect organisation may also be gradually induced, developed in course of time. This plasticity or modifiability of man assures us that if the efforts of education to rectify humanity be properly directed, they will not be in vain. Education, therefore, may be considered, when exercising its true functions, as the greatest, the most important of the formative arts.

For these reasons, we prefer applying to education the analogies to be drawn from the sculptor's art rather than those which may be derived from husbandry; the thorough formative sense of *re-modelling*, re-moulding, to that of *cultivation*. This is warranted, too, by the Parable of the Potter. The potter forms his vessels of clay, to honour or dishonour, according as he is either a good or a bad workman; so does the good or bad educator. The objects of the statuary and the educator are very analogous. In the one case it is the lifeless, in the other the living clay which has to be conformed to the ideal. But the living human organism and form can only be perfected by right reason and knowledge working from within, and controlling vital action. The true educator, therefore, commences the re-moulding of man by first rectifying the understanding, and placing before it the *pattern* or *ideal* standard, which he, in common with the sculptor, desires to realise, but in this case palpitating with the breath of life. The true educator should possess a Phidian mastery over human intellect, organisation, and form.

Socrates, through his father's occupation, may have owed some of his power over men to his detection of the analogy between the two formative arts, and we have seen it somewhere stated that the *Veda* predicts that, 'The ultimate reformation of mankind is to proceed from a teacher or master of Art.' It is remarkable too, that a tradition exists that the carpenter's shop at Nazareth, was not strictly that in the modern sense, but rather of a sculptor or figure maker. This receives some colour of probability from the use of the term *carpenter* in a particular verse of Isaiah (xliv. 13). These fanciful speculations, however, are merely cited to show that a certain affinity has been perceived to exist between the arts of sculpture and education, and that the forming of living men, as of statues, is a plastic art. We shall now proceed to consider the transfer of power in the human system.

CHAPTER III.

THE TRANSFER OF POWER FROM ONE PART OF THE SYSTEM TO ANOTHER.—A BALANCED OR EQUABLE DISTRIBUTION OF POWER AMONGST THE FACULTIES TO BE AIMED AT.

THE modifiability of human nature, of which we have just treated, necessarily includes the transfer of power from one function, or set of functions, to others, or no remoulding of either congenital or induced disproportion could be effected. We find in man, indeed, the organic structure adapted for the greatest variety of transfer of power. It is true that many of the *Mammalia* are so constituted as greatly to excel man in particular kinds of locomotion; but we shall in vain look for the same combination and mastery of his powers which the erect posture implies. The monkey climbs and jumps with a facility truly extraordinary, but it is with difficulty, or only for a short time, that he raises himself into the erect position. Dogs, horses, deer, excel man in swiftness, but they cannot climb or walk erect. The otter, the beaver, and the seal swim well, but it is their only advantage above creatures of their own kind; and whales, or other cetaceous animals, though admirably adapted for swimming, have no other mode of locomotion.   Man, on the other hand, stands, and walks erect, runs, jumps, climbs, swims.   Man, alone, can so modify his frame, that it is in his power to waive the high privilege of the harmony and balance of his faculties, and by concentrating his volition to any one property or perfection, we have reason to believe that he might equal or excel the beast most characterized by that perfection—outrun the deer, outwrestle the bear, climb with the monkey.   In short, man has the most modifiable organs of motion, and is most capable of subjugating them to his will, and of rendering them the instruments of his varied purposes.   We had, in a former treatise, recourse to the *argumentum ad adsurdum* to prove that if the moral form of humanity be not an aggregation of moderate powers ; that if the regal or ideal manhood be not the balanced proportioned nature indicated, it must inhere in inequality and disproportion, some irregular, quantitative relation of excess and defect, which is contrary to common sense.   Now the formative laws enunciated, while they point to the equable or average distribution of vital power between the faculties as the condition of the perfection of human life, infer the possible existence of a very opposite state, or the monopoly of power by special functions to the detriment of others, and that either of these states may be induced ; in the one case by a judicious, in the other injudicious, transfer of power; although in either case its sum total may be considered as remaining a constant quantity,

Having stated the theory of the distribution of vitality to obtain balanced functional power, we turn to consider the consequences of educating according to the opposite formative principle, or the development of special faculties. It is very evident that every faculty cannot have the whole vitality; this must be simultaneously shared either equally or unequally, or be transferred to one or the other at different times: and it is between the system of the monopoly, or distribution, of vital power in the human system that education has to decide. In ignorance of the limits of the power of the human constitution, you will find men destroying themselves by acting as if it were possible to do everything at once, and who therefore may be compared to pyres lighted in several places, which are soon consumed, or who are, by a more vulgar comparison, said 'to burn the candle at both ends.'

That the transfer of power to special functions is possible; that one portion of the system may be aggrandised at the expense of another; that some faculties may be abnormally developed by the dwarfing of others, is evident from our everyday experience of the principle of allowing the strongest natural bias to have its way, and become overwhelmingly predominant. And recollect, this is the educational doctrine to which we, as a nation, still say; 'Laissez faire'! Of course from such a doctrine various forms of gross excentration result, incapacitating men, more or less, for the general conduct of affairs, for the complete circle of social existence. This excentration may be observed in members of various liberal professions, as well as in athletes, gluttons, and sensualists, all of whom exhibit some abnormal activity or excess in some special direction, and of course a corresponding weakness or defect. Society exclusively composed of such special functioned men could never cohere. The mystic is either too chimerical or sedentary for the practicalness and energy required in public life. The glutton, because incompetent in most things, the amassing of wealth and hatred of genius excepted. The sensualist, because careless to everything but his own gratification. The athletes, because indifferent to intellectual culture and their tendency to solve everything by a word and a blow; and some poets, painters, literary men and musicians, because they think their own vocations the worthiest and best, the only true end of being, and consequently, that they may dispense with all other considerations, may exhibit an utter indifference to all mundane affairs which have no immediate relation to their adopted specialities. We very well know that in these cases the patients are quite oblivious to, quite unconscious of, their onesidedness; that they are cripples both in their aspirations, and mental organisation ; and that they fail in that healthy balanced nature which characterizes genius.*

This is the fault of wrong leading, of wrong training—is for want of a right educational *setting up* in early life, if not the result of some congenital constitutional defect. For it may readily be conceded that disproportionate, imperfect, organisation may be inherited as well as induced ; nevertheless this must have been initiated somewhen in the past, by some ill treatment, some wrong direction of the humanity. And if this be true we may moralize for a moment on the dread legacy, of pains and penalties, which may ensue from perverting the symmetry of organisation. This consideration ought to form a strong incentive to correct inherited defects, to remould humanity by judicious training to true symmetry. But whether defects be either inherited, or superinduced, there are the disproportioned natures, exceeding in some respects and falling short in others of the ideal standard, by thousands and tens of thousands, and who demanding our admiration for the something more, would crave our pity for the something less, could we always probe their weaknesses.

If the sacrifice of a part of our nature be purposely and deliberately made for some great end, the sacri-

---

* As a rule, the greatest men are not one-functioned men, but men of large general powers.

fice it is held demands our admiration, but here it is difficult to weigh advantage against disadvantage; for it should be borne in mind that the aggrandisement of special functions at the expense of others is rather in the quantity than the quality of the function increased, for the power being turned all to one side, it loses something by the perversion of its relation to the larger and truer humanity. And in this case we should have to forego a fixed for a variable system of morality, for if we reflect it will soon be perceived, that the very object of ethics is to fix a standard to which all men should be conformed. In the voluntary transfer and monopoly of power by special functions, there is this inevitable result to be looked for, viz., that when those faculties, to which the vital power has been undividedly directed through a long period of time, begin to exhibit symptoms of wear and tear, of exhaustion and decay, those kept in abeyance will reassert themselves—a change sometimes leading to gratifying, at others to deplorable results.

As, therefore, we cannot keep the whole of our powers at full work at one and the same time, nor transfer power to special functions through long periods of time without producing mischievous results, a temporary and alternate transfer of power to special faculties would appear to be the most economical and wisest mode of using vitality, if circumstances prevent equable life.

All training for either mental or physical *tours de force* is essentially a temporary transfer of power to special faculties for some special and determinate end ; but it is abnormal, and cannot be prolonged beyond the premonitory symptoms of nature's inclination to fall back without injury to the system. A man in training is not in perfect health, for there is always a suppression of power in some direction that it may be thrown into another. Similar principles to those adopted to produce high muscularity, may by different direction produce high intellectuality, and are attended by similar dangers. The Greeks thoroughly understood all these matters, and aimed at that physical and intellectual balance which is alone the condition of health and beauty. As for some years after maturity the system is quickly recuperative, has an abundant supply of vitality, athletics, as society is at present constituted, are perhaps the best safety-valve ; but the super-abundant vitality could just as well and as safely be turned into mental gymnastics. But men are as yet too ignorant upon these matters to understand the full bearing and import of what we say, or to put a favourable construction on a man who intellectually trains himself to serve his country, instead of rowing a four-mile race.

It is found that nature compensates the congenitally or accidentally maimed by this very process of transfer, the blind by increased sensitiveness of touch, the deaf and dumb by keen sight and sensitiveness to motion ; and to effect a similar transfer for some special and important end, without really maiming ourselves, we must suppress sometimes one, sometimes another portion of our nature.

Dietetics when raised to the dignity of a science will doubtless render important aid towards symmetrical development, not only by setting forth the quantities and qualities of foods best adapted to different ages, but also those which best fit a man for special purposes. During childhood and youth a larger proportion of food is requisite to support the growth of the body than after maturity when the frame has attained its full growth. For some years after maturity there is abundant energy, the vital power wells up and can meet considerable calls upon it, can be considerably taxed and with comparative impunity. At this period athletics may be freely encouraged as long as it is steadfastly kept in mind that they must not be pursued to the tension of straining, for if they are permanent injury will be the consequence. Dietetics as a science, too, will furnish us with valuable information as to the graduated regimen adapted to the various periods of, and calculated to prolong life ; as to the importance of dispensing with the ' fire-waters ' till the lamp of life is getting low, and the mischief inevitably attendant on adding this fuel to the volcanic fires of youth.

How could a despotism most effectually enthral a nation and set its heel upon its neck? Why! by promoting every kind of one-sidedness, by directing men's minds exclusively to specialities and technicalities, and by these means gradually diverting their mental and physical organisation from the true standard, and thus disqualifying them for true citizenship. And it is even within the bounds of possibility that such a government, in its treachery and cowardice, might contemplate and be proud of its nation of slaves. Workmen! if you desire political power, keep the principle of 'symmetry' in education steadfastly in view.

We have previously stated that a system of morals infers the possibility of making the constitution of men uniform, or approximately uniform, but as this uniformity does not at present exist, we have to believe that it will, or the moral law would be a dead letter. The individuation of men, indeed, is in direct opposition to the principle of moral unification and at-one-ment; it tends to preserve, or rather to widen, the difference between man and man, and to make obedience to one code more and more difficult. In whatever way the argument is logically treated the clearer does it become manifest that the true mission of education is to take advantage of the plasticity or modifiability of human nature and to mould it to a true standard. The consideration of the subject of the transfer of power may have shown more completely than the direct course of argument that the balanced manhood should be the ideal of the educator ; this which has been variously designated the *mean*, the *average*, the *central*, the *moral* and the ideal form of man, may also be styled the regal manhood. Dr. Johnson defines genius as a mind of large general powers accidentally directed to some particular object. Now the *mean* or essential manhood is that, which, take it all in all, must have the largest *general* power, and which being observant on all sides and well poised will be most alive to everything affecting a special subject,* and never drag it into the mire of one-sided-ness, into the estrangement of isolation, as bias does, but builds it up aright now, and for all time. The regal manhood would be great in any class, in any-thing—the most efficient workman. Here the con-clusions of science stop, and it may perhaps, from some recent observations, be erroneously supposed that the spirit of self sacrifice is to be excluded from consideration. The conclusions of science with regard to the ideal are in strict conformity with religious teaching, but the progress of humanity

---

* The symmetrical form is always the largest containing in proportion to its boundary.

does not yet maintain an even tenor. There is so much to be done, so much to be amended and effected by compromise during a state of transition, that Christianity comes to our aid with its high motive of self sacrifice, when this can be conscientiously offered for the commonweal, for some great end. But this must be the result of a deliberate and wise discretion that the good to be thus purchased be of greater value than the sacrifice. And do not think self sacrifice is uncommon ; for self sacrifice is of two kinds, that which sacrifices the worse to the better nature, the other the better to the worse: of this latter and impious kind there is all too much, but for the former there is yet the occasion, the work.

Hitherto, we have but broadly indicated the nature of the ideal to which humanity should be conformed ; but now proceed to consider it in detail.

CHAPTER IV.

THE RIGHT CONSTITUTION OF THE PREPARATORY OR EDUCATIONAL SETTING-UP SCHOOLS OF THE KINGDOM.

IT has been stated that the last International Exhibition in Paris convinced competent observers that English workmen are less skilful than the continental; not as our kind and considerate censors inform us, from any irremediable defect in the English artizan's nature, but in default of an organized system of Technical Training. This is very remarkable, for so much has since been done in that direction. In 1851 we were told that the British workman was far ahead of all others in every department but the art-manufactures, and now, after a considerable lapse of time, in which greater facilities have been afforded for technical study, we are told that he is behind the foreign workman in every kind of handicraft. This is by no means either encouraging or consoling, and is so opposite to the result predicted that we begin to suspect that the 'cry' for Technical Instruction is a mistake, and that where we are really at fault is in our general system of education; that it is in this that some radical change is required. And not only do we believe that the 'cry' for Technical Education is a great mistake, and very impolitic, but that its agitation is directly mischievous to the true interests of education by diverting public attention from the real source of mischief: the deep rooted defects of our general system of education. And the reader will perhaps the more readily believe that this is written in no partisan spirit when he is informed that we were the first to put forth a plan for a grand Central Polytechnic College at South Kensington in 1851.

The Englishman owes so much to steam that if it be suggested that there is something at fault in our system of education, his first impulse and conclusion is that it does not yet admit sufficient instruction in science and mechanism, and forthwith insists that schools and colleges ought to be converted into workshops. Never was there a mistake more fatal in its tendency to the best interests of the country, more calculated to subvert our prestige as manufacturers. We believe the country's deficiency in this respect is exaggerated, misrepresented. England has already the best of all technical schools—her workshops. The studio, the office, the workshop, are the proper places for this kind of instruction. But of late years the ruling notion of an Englishman in reference to an improvement in our educational system has been that machinery should be thrust before every child's eyes, and hammers, saws, and chisels put into every boy's hands.

Museums of inventions exhibiting every kind of mechanical contrivance and manufacturing process are to a cerain extent valuable, interesting, and instructive, and afford the inventor the opportunity of ascertaining what has already been done, nevertheless their utility is very limited, more useful we believe to amateur mechanicians, who frequently waste their time in re-inventing things half a century old, than practical men. The practical or professional inventor is *au courant* of the times in these matters, conversant with existing imperfections in mechanical arrangements, or some want to be supplied. But before allowing ourselves to dwell too exclusively on the importance of establishing technical institutions, there is a matter of far greater import to be attended to, viz. the establishment of schools to develope the workman's faculties, to make him rational, true sighted, and dextrous handed. This accomplished, we might proceed to found poly-technic museums. But the right development of the man should be our first and chiefest solicitude. If the knowledge of mechanics, hydrostatics, pneumatics chemistry, geology, &c., essentially contributed to make the skilful workman, and to stamp a nation's art with genius, how is it that the Greeks and the Italians produced the most exquisite workmanship— work which we, scientific people that we are, can as yet scarcely imitate, much less excel? It is well known that the great masterpieces of art and manufacture, some of which are now treasured and exhibited as examples, were produced without that scientific and technical training which it is now the fashion to insist on.

The greatest philosophers, poets, dramatists, architects, statesmen, and generals the world has yet seen, owed scarcely anything to the study of the physical sciences, and yet they were not inferior in intellect, in manhood, on this account. It is clear, therefore, that these studies are not of the first importance in forming men. The sciences are only so many different branches of enquiry requiring the self-same essential mental powers to be brought to bear upon them, as those more important to human culture. Ages since, a people entirely without polytechnic museums, national galleries, &c., produced the finest painting, sculpture, architecture, gems and ceramic ware the world as ever seen, and yet we persist in regarding means they never adopted as absolutely essential to the attainment of the same excellence.

The English are truly a strange people, proud of their originality, and original their devices certainly are, for raising the general intelligence of the people. The importance of technical institutions on the Continent may easily be accounted for; there workshops had to be created, the manufactures to be forced, in order to compete with the longer established industrial organisation of England.

The whole tendency of the technical system is to specialise and reduce men to mere machines ; and to specialise is, as we have already shown, to narrow the sphere of vital action ; for there are but two possible tendencies in nature, viz., either to excentration or symmetry, either to the unbalanced or the balanced ; the eccentric, the unbalanced, the disproportionate are but different expressions for *special* development. The two opposite tendencies may be thus formulated :—

1. Beings in which the greatest number of faculties are concentrated in their mean or moderate degree of development, manifest the largest *general* powers.

2. Beings in which any special faculty, or group of faculties, are inordinately developed, exhibit some *special* aptitude, but are deficient in *varied* mobility, in *general* capacity. Their *specialisation* increasing as the excentration or disproportion constituting their individuality or characteristic increases.

Now, if the full import of these two positions be thoroughly grasped, the title ‘ Proportionate or Symmetrical System ’ will at once be understood, indicating, as it does, a system essentially opposed to that which has so long been in vogue, viz., that based upon the misconceptions that *bias* in the human character should be cultivated, and that quantity and variety of knowledge are preferable to quality in education, to the regulated, symmetrical cultivation of the whole manhood.

If the popular notions on the subject of education be examined, it will be found that they are, in the main, founded on phrenology; and under the supposition that this is a sound theory of the constitution of the mind, when it is nothing but a mere shaky hypothesis; hence tendencies in character resulting from accident and habit are attributed to the promptings of certain cerebral organs. These organs, confidently mapped out, are so numerous that it can scarcely be wondered if teachers and parents, whose notions are derived from phrenology, should be anxious to 'cram' youth with all kinds of information, lest it should appear naturally deficient, *minus* any cerebral protuberances. Hence one of the principal motives to 'cramming,' and the origin of the absurd notion of the great variety of study necessary to develope the intellect. This is, indeed, one of the most absurd and fatal mistakes of modern times, and is as injurious to mental development as 'cramming' the stomach is to digestion; the healthy action of the mind, as of the body, is impossible under such treatment.

Everyone is aware that what is rapidly learned—that is merely committed to memory—is very commonly forgotten as quickly, 'one set of ideas driving out another.' That thorough apprehension of what is learned, on the other hand, by which it is made (as it were) part of the mental fabric, is a much slower process. The difference between the two is expressed by the colloquial term 'cramming,' as distinguished from 'learning'; the analogy being obvious to the overloading the stomach with a mass of food too great to be digested aud assimilated within a given time, so that a large part of it passes *out of* the body without having been applied to any good purpose *in* it. A part of this difference obviously consists in the formation of *mental associations* between the newly acquired knowledge and that previously possessed; so that the new ideas become linked on with the old by 'suggesting' chains. Such is especially the case when we are applying ourselves to the study of any branch of knowledge, with the view of permanently mastering it; and here the element of *time* is found practically to be very important. Thus it is recorded of the late Lord St. Leonards, that having (as Sir Edward Sugden) been asked by Sir T. F. Buxton what was the secret of his success, his answer was,— 'I resolved, when beginning to read law, to make everything I acquired *perfectly my own*, and never to go to a second thing till I had entirely accomplished the first. Many of my competitors read as much in a day as I read in a week; but at the end of twelve months my knowledge was as fresh as on the day it was acquired, whilst theirs had glided away from their recollection ('Memoirs of Sir T. F. Buxton,' chap. xxiv.) In this assimilating process, it is obvious that the new knowledge is (as it were) turned over and over in the mind, and viewed in all its aspects; so that by its coming to be, not merely an *addition* to the old, but to *interpenetrate* it, the old can scarcely be brought into the "sphere of consciousness," without bringing the new with it.'*

The proportionate or Symmetrical system of Education we are now advocating is based on that great and immutable science of definite proportional relation which obtains throughout the Cosmos. The leading positions of this doctrine, applicable to the subject in hand, may be thus stated :—

1. That all wrong, imperfection, disproportion, are aberrations from *mean*, or *average* conditions. The mean, therefore, is the common measure of rectitude in all things, of the proportioned, the symmetrical, of the good, the perfect, the beautiful.

2. That any *special* excess in any system of being, necessarily involves a *special* defect: this results from a transfer or excentration of power.

3. That as the vitality or power in any system of being is a *fixed* quantity, any excessive expenditure of vitality, by one function or group of functions, must be compensated by inaction in others; or by the

* 'On Acquired Physical Habits,' by Dr. W. B. Carpenter.

system generally, by a period of absolute rest ; otherwise organisation will be impaired, the common store of vitality unduly drawn upon, and existence shortened. This expounds the great law of Compensation, by which irregular activity in body or mind may be corrected and health restored.

That any *special excess* or any system of being necessarily involves a *special defect*, at once indicates the weakness of the educational system which would promote or develope *bias*. For it will at once be seen by (2) that any special aptitude of mind or body can only be developed at the expense of its proportion, its symmetry. The general efficiency of the humanity is impaired by such a course. The truth of this position is, in fact, frequently attested by the exclamation 'O yes ! he is very clever in that way, but a fool in respect to everything else.' That we have a public superficially informed, crochetty, excentric, incapable of observing or reasoning correctly, thinking deeply or seeing far ahead, is due to the absurd system of developing *bias*.

The cultivation of *bias*, of special intellectual or physical idiosyncrasies, inevitably tends to foster and increase what is evidently by (2) a predominance or disproportion in the man, and, therefore to destroy that proportion or symmetry in which well-being consists, or that regal manhood which is neither in excess nor defect of anything essentially human.

We may perceive too that nature may be broadly divided into the right and the wrong; and that the wrong is so, because it is either in *excess* or *defect* of what it should be, or the right. Of the right alone can it not be said that it has in any respect too much, or not enough. In the ratio, therefore, in which a human being falls short of the symmetrical, regal, or ideal manhood will he, if it be on the intellectual side, be erratic, eccentric, paradoxical, if on the sensual side, troublesome, burthensome, or dangerous.

The three phases of life to which men have to be educated are the political, the social, and the professional or technical; but the true education for the political life may be said, if not to include the others, to be the best preparation for them ; for to exercise the rights of citizenship in the highest acceptation of that word, requires the largest general powers, that proportionate or symmetrical development of the man now advocated. The *regal* manhood is *socially* the best, for as men become more perfected in their general nature are their affections and tastes compelled to move in unison with it. The regal manhood is also professionally the best, for it regards its *special* vocation from all sides, is above clique, fashion, mannerism, or pettiness. The true education for the political life, or for citizenship, begets, in short, that co-ordination of the entire nature which confers mastery, and rightly governs the social and professional phases of being.

E

An hypothesis, though perchance erroneous, may serve as a parade ground on which facts may be marshalled ; but this, which it is our vocation to uphold, leads to such a multitude of common sense conclusions, and enables us to unravel so much that was previously entangled, as to convince us, as similar principles did Humboldt, that we grasp principles of sublime simplicity and certainty. Those who accept the proportional theory of education, may perhaps, for some time yet be ridiculed as *doctrinaires*, but as no one can expect to be practically useful unless he first be theoretically correct, we must still cogitate and await the verdict of the future.

The title proportionate or symmetrical may be too general for the apprehension of the ordinary reader ; we must, therefore, descend further into exposition and detail, but before doing this, we would direct the reader's attention to that portion of our essay which demonstrated that human nature, mental and physical, is plastic and modifiable : this was a necessary preliminary, for if human nature were not plastic, it would be in vain to attempt the regeneration of mankind. All schemes for improving the moral, intellectual, or physical status of mankind are framed upon the tacit conviction that human, like other nature, is modifiable ; divertible from, and convertible to the highest type of well-being: Education, then, is essentially a formative art; as essentially so as the plastic arts, commonly so called, and though its finished work may require a much longer period to accomplish than the painter or sculptor's, it will, when it shall be invested with full powers and in the plenitude of its mastery, be able to develop whatever *manner of man* it wills. It will be by this time fully evident that, in accordance with our primary confession, we have been driving full tilt against the vulgar error, that cultivating and still further exaggerating ' the *natural* bias,' as it is termed, is the true mode of educating. Only attempt to carry out this notion in imagination, thoroughly and consistently in *all* cases of *natural bias*, whether good or bad, and you will be completely convinced that it is wrong. The strongest natural bias is always impatient of bit and curb: but give it head and spur and it clean bolts with a man. The true object of education is, on the contrary, and as we have already stated, to strengthen by every means in our power those faculties and powers which are defective or imperfectly developed. Both the intellect and physique according to the principle enunciated (3) page (47) draw upon a common fund of vitality of which the prodigal expenditure by either disturbs and injures the desirable balance and healthy tone of the system. And not only is this the case in respect to the general equipoise of mind and body, but if any functional power in either be excessively or extravagantly used, in short, any disproportionate organisation or activity in

E 2

any portion or function of the system destroys the just temper and perfect harmony of its well-being. Lord Macaulay, when writing of the men of a certain eventful period of our history, says, 'The constitution of their mind was remarkably sound. No *particular* faculty was *pre-eminently* developed, but manly health and vigour were equally diffused through the whole.' Or as Shakespeare says, 'The elements were so *mixed* in them that nature might stand up and say— These were men!' Now this 'equable' development, these 'elements so mixed in them,' are but different modes of expressing the symmetrical or proportionate constitution, that aggregation or concentration of moderate qualities indicated in the middle column of the annexed table. Such an aggregation is, indeed, the rational analysis of the ideal or regal manhood, which a true system of education should keep steadfastly in view as its 'pattern.' It is, indeed, that average, essential, and symmetrical manhood divested of all the accidents of eccentricity or aberration. Yet, strange to say, we may very frequently hear of this average[1] or symmetrically constituted man, being jauntily asked for, as if he were a common and a very easily to be obtained commodity, ready to answer and flock to advertisement by the thousand. Why it is this 'manner of man,' he in whom no *particular* faculty is

---

[1] The truth is the *average man*, in common parlance, means a mediocrity either on the side of *excess* or *defect*, and not that true *central* form alluded to.

pre-eminently developed, but the whole manhood, in its mean, symmetrical, or moderate degree, who has been in all times the true genius, reformer, and deliverer. He, of all men, is the most remote from the Simian type; he, of all men, the least likely to damage or wreck a good cause. It is because society is a conglomerate of disproportioned humanity, that the State has to assume the functions of the regal manhood, and by this mean endeavour to harmonise and balance the body politic.

Table of Means and Extremes.

EXTREME BY EXCESS.	MEAN OF RECTITUDE. THE ELEMENTS OF THE SYMMETRICAL IDEAL.	EXTREME BY DEFECT.
Intemperate	Moderate	Abstinent
Tyrannical	Magnanimous	Mean
—	Just	—
Rash	Courageous	Timid
Extravagant	Liberal	Parsimonious
Credulous	Trustful	Suspicious
Licentious	Free	Austere
Assurance	Confidence	False Modesty
Boisterous	Good-humored	Dull
'Fast'	Even-tenored	'Slow'
Quick	Gentle	Immobile
Passionate	Attempered	Cold
Fastidious	Refined	Coarse
Facile	Firm	Obstinate
Reckless	Prudent	Over-wistful
—	Discreet	—

Table of Means and Extremes—continued.

Tending to develope respectively—

EXTREME BY EXCESS.	MEAN OF RECTITUDE. THE ELEMENTS OF THE SYMMETRICAL IDEAL.	EXTREME BY DEFECT.
Disproportion	The Symmetrical, Beautiful, or Moral form	Disproportion
Dwarfed forms and features	Average forms and features	Dwarfed forms and features

HABITS TENDING TO DISEASE, DEFORM; TO SHORTEN EXISTENCE.	HABITS TENDING TO PRESERVE HEALTH AND BEAUTY.	HABITS TENDING TO DISEASE, DEFORM; TO SHORTEN EXISTENCE.
Excessive exercise	Moderate exercise	Insufficient exercise
Excessive exercise of any function, mental or physical	Moderate or moral use of any function, mental or physical	Insufficient use of any function, mental or physical
Excessive eating and drinking; gluttony	Moderation	Abstinence, long fasting, insufficient food

We have now to point out how the symmetrical or proportionate system of education is to be conducted: how this regal or symmetrical manhood we have so often spoken of, and which the Greeks appear to have so thoroughly understood, is to be developed. Not, as we have already shown, by the cultivation of *bias* in either mind or body. Not by excessive exercise of the mind to the depression of the body, nor of the body to the detriment of the mind. But by an equable, temperate exercise of the whole being, if naturally well-proportioned ; or if disproportioned, by a careful attention to, and exercise of, the defective faculties. Let us descend somewhat farther into particulars, and endeavour to clear our minds on the subject of the faculties of the mind, and from the embar-rassment of those numerous ones with which phre-nology accredits us. To do this methodically and successfully, we must have regard to the order in which we receive impressions from the external world. Let us, therefore, trace the natural sequence of our knowledge of the external world from our first im-pressions, or facts, to understanding. These facts, or first impressions, are derived from the outpost obser-vant senses ; secondly, they are registered in memory, and, thirdly, they are ordered, systematised, and util-ised by reason. The mind is constituted of the receptive, retaining, and digestive faculties ; and its healthy action is dependent on the perfection, and proper balance, and interdependence of these three faculties either being maintained or developed. For if the senses be imperfectly educated or developed, men will be bad observers, the memory full of false entries ; and reason, having false data, will be impeded in its attempts to arrive at just conclusions. And the importance of properly training the senses must presently be enlarged upon. According to our primary position (2), page (47), the three powers or faculties of observation, memory, and reason should be of an equally proportioned or balanced excellence. For if the power of observation be cultivated to the neglect of the retaining and reasoning faculties, there will be a clinging to mere facts and minutiæ, a too facile credulity, disconnected thought, uncertain and inconsistent action. If the memory or retaining faculty be stimulated to excess, and burdened with an encyclopædic store of information, it will be at the expense of the observing and reasoning faculties, and there will be a loquacity on all subjects, and a facile power of dispensing second-hand knowledge; but should originality be attempted by this disproportioned intellectual constitution, its data will be incorrect, its conclusions false. If the reasoning faculty, on the other hand, be unduly exercised to the detriment of the healthy activity of observation and memory, it will not only be at fault in its premises, but fruitful in reckless hypotheses, systematically wrong. The moral form or right constitution and interdependence of the three faculties of observation, memory, and reason is when they are duly proportioned to each other, *symmetrically* co-ordinated; and when thus constituted the intellect is organically perfect, fitted to investigate nature, to discover or confirm truth. What subject is there that these three faculties are not competent to grapple with, be it religious, ethical, political, educational, physical, artistic, linguistic, or any other; in short, within the sphere of the knowable?   They are the three central essential faculties of the intellect, which, when properly proportioned, give mastery over any subject on which they are brought to bear.

Preserving this idea of proportion, symmetry, or balance, and keeping it steadfastly in the mind's eye as expressing the constitution of the ideal or regal manhood, of the right constitution of the moral, intellectual, and physical man, it will be perceived to be of the utmost importance that the studies essentially necessary to that ideal development should be rescued from that *entourage* of considerations by which they are now kept out of view, and their intrinsic importance lost sight of, and made the basis of our educational system.   The provision for amplifications, specialities, and superfluities is of secondary consideration.   These essential studies should constitute the curriculum of the Setting-Up education of the country—of the 'Setting-Up schools,' as we would call them, instead of ' Primary.' These basic or fundamental subjects are comprised under the following six heads:— 1. Self-government.   2. The Observing Faculty.   3. The Retaining Faculty, or Memory.   4. The Rational Faculty.   5. The means of communicating knowledge.   6. The Physique. These, the six points of the Charta of Education, may be thus formulated :—

The Six Points.

1. Self-government—Ethics
   - Religion.
   - Scientific Ethics.
   - The Laws of Health.

2. The Observing Faculty—Art.
   - Drawing or Modelling.
   - Music.
   - Geography.
   - Writing.

3. The Memory or the Retaining Faculty
   - By judicious exercise upon all the subjects studied.

4. The Rational Faculty—Mathematics
   - Arithmetic.
   - Algebra.
   - Geometry.

5. The means of communicating knowledge } Language . The National Language.

6. The Physique—Gymnastics
   - By various exercises of the body.

It will be scarcely necessary to enlarge upon the importance of points 1, 3, 4, and 5; but on points 2 and 6, The Training of the Observing Faculty and The Physique, we have something to say. The importance of training or educating the senses will become more evident if we reflect that it is from impressions received through the eye and the ear that we are enabled to bear witness to what is passing in the external world; and teachers of drawing and music only fully know what false witnesses these senses are before they are properly trained. Let it not be forgotten, too, that it is upon the testimony of these two, commonly uncultivated, senses that character and life are frequently at stake.

The desire to obey the command, 'Thou shalt not bear false witness,' may sometimes be strengthened, but evidence cannot be guaranteed upon oath. If a witness be an imperfect observer by eye or ear, and such a one he commonly is, in default of the educational training on which we are now insisting, he may quite conscientiously swear to the absolute truth of his false impressions. There is an art teacher who frequently points this moral in his class: ' If,' says he to his pupils, 'you misapprehend the truth with regard to the model immediately before you, and biding your time for deliberate inspection, how can you expect to observe and remember correctly the moving scenes and occurrences of everyday life?' It is, however, not only in the witness-box that trained senses are required, but for the recognition and appreciation of beauty in nature, to preside watchfully over all kinds of work, and to endow the art and manufactures of a nation with that permanent excellence which will ensure their appreciation throughout the civilised world. We are speaking more immediately of the education of the eye. And we will venture to predict that you would find that painters and sculptors could be more. readily converted, or their hands turned, to any other kind of work than any other man in the community: and why? Not solely because their arts require the greatest dexterity of hand, but because they have educated eyes and can see better. Depend upon it, all the study of the physical sciences at present advocated will not do half so much for the workshops of England as teaching drawing, modelling, and music in schools. The study of the physical sciences may facilitate invention, extend our sway over means, but does only in a very slight and almost inappreciable degree contribute to the development of the student's nature, and more especially as the knowledge of these is generally got up by 'cram.' And when we propose a course of art in all the setting-up schools of the queendom we do not mean that it is to be treated as an inessential, and with indignity, as it often is, in the schools and colleges of England ; but as one of the essentials of a true education, of that education which alone deserves the title of liberal. Not as a study which may be followed in inconvenient and ill-lighted class rooms, furnished with a dirty cast or two, and a few half-obliterated flat copies; but as one to be pursued in class rooms specially designed and lighted for the purpose, well found in the best examples of art and as a study which should have a fair share of every day's time devoted to it. We cannot so well speak from experience of what is requisite for the due study of music, but this should also be as carefully provided for. Think of the effect which such a training would have upon taste, and consequently upon the arts and manufactures of the country. What new and healthful source of recreation it would open to the workman; and how in a short time it would raise the whole status of art, for as the toe of the artizan gibed the heels of the painter and sculptor, these would be compelled to stride forward.

The other subject on which we proposed to enlarge was (6) or the Training of the Physique. Work of some kinds is in itself a healthy exercise; there are other kinds, however, which demand considerable muscular activity, but at the same time necessitate some list of the body, some cramped position, by no means calculated to preserve health or develop true symmetry of form; and the deforming tendencies of such adverse conditions might be neutralised by judicious gymnastic training. The value of exercise and gymnastic training is great, not only in the interests of health and form, but of defence; for we have to remember that in the present state of the world we have still to be militant. The institutions most dear to us, and the work of progress, may yet be forcibly assailed, and to meet and repel such an assault we must be men physically as well as mentally. We shall by-and-by learn too, that beauty, symmetry of form, is the outward and unmistakeable sign of a healthy, progressive, and noble people. The conversion of a people from irregular, immoral life, does, as it progresses, restore beauty to a people; the change from ugliness and deformity may be slow, but it is

sure, and is a truth which was recognised ages since.
Can the deformation and decadence of human nature
proceed from anything but erratic action, from other
than ill-governed, ill-regulated, vital action ? The
inevitable result of irregular action in mechanism is
well known.   Can we feel surprised then if the mar-
vellously delicate structures and organs of the living
body are grievously injured by reckless and immo-
derate use ? A variety of evil influences tend to
shake the nerves, dwarf the body, deform the limbs,
and distort the features in the present day.   English
life is socially morbid ; we have long been unwhole-
somely stimulated by a love of riches, ambition :
wealth and power, at any cost, has been our resolve.
Disorganisation has set in, as a natural consequence,
and must continue, till we are guided by those higher
motives which produce remedial re-action.

Physical training has in England never been wholly
disregarded as one of the elements of education. But
of late years too much importance has been attached
to it, and like all English hobbies it has been ridden
to ridiculous excess.   The use of gymnastic exercise
requires considerable judgment and scientific direction. The doctrine of proportion supplies us with 'the
measure of that stature and fulness,' of that symmetry
in which health and beauty inhere ; that golden mean,
in which there is neither excess nor defect.   The
mean is the measure of that ideal to which men are

gradually 'to go on, and grow up unto,' by the moral or just use of every function of their being : mind dominating, conforming, co-ordinating the entire nature—with this immutable measure in our possession, there will be no danger of muscularity being over-developed for the sake of being stronger for mischief, or for those purposes which so long prejudiced and degraded athletic exercises. In the training the body, the law we have already formulated must never be lost sight of, viz., that as vitality is a fixed quantity, 'no one faculty, or group of faculties, can be excessively exercised and developed, but at the expense of others'—prodigious mental activity will be at the cost of the body, great muscular effort by a diminution of intellectual activity ; and if vital power be continuously diverted in one direction, abnormal organisation and deformation ensue. The great danger to be guarded against, then, in the institution of gymnastics and athletics as a branch of general education is, lest their true limits should be overstepped, and an excessive development of thew and sinew be thought their right aim ; lest that *moral form* be lost sight of in which all the faculties are co-ordinated, and from which excentration or aberration implies deformation and predisposition to disease. Rewards should never be offered for excessive feats of strength, but for general capacity, mental and physical. It would be of far greater advantage to human progress to crown

symmetry, instead of prodigious feats of strength.
The Greeks, above all other people, best understood
the training of men, and consequently those proportions in which beauty inheres. They had intellectual
as well as physical symmetry in view in the institution
of their Olympic Games, which had a dignity of purpose that never ennobled the Roman games, never
sanctified the amphitheatres wherein men, brutalised
by strength, contended with brutes. The foregoing
observations are the more necessary, as we have lately
seen the form of the Farnese Hercules, with the
legend, *Mens sana in corpore sano*, adopted as the
device and heading of the circulars of an Athletic
Association. Now the Farnese Hercules, as sculptors
well know, is an embodiment of physical excess, a
mountain of muscle capped by a weak summit. Such
an embodiment is wide of the mark of true manly
beauty, of that mid-form in which all the faculties of
mind and body are duly apportioned. The '*mens
sana*' would be morally impossible in an incarnation
of the Hercules; such a being, from his mental immobility, would only be a club-bearer and slave. The
true intellectual and physical conformation of man is
doubtless that increasing purpose which is widening
with the process of the suns. We see what frightful
decadence in human form and intellect may be produced by wrong direction through time; let us try
what can be done towards restoration by an opposite

course; we know too what vast changes can be effected for the better in other forms of being when man is intent upon moulding them to his own purposes.

Let us, then, devote our great knowledge and energies to the Restoration of men, intellectually, morally, and physically. It takes a long time to learn how to be and to be men. But if our energies and knowledge be rightly applied, we need not despair of ultimate success. Seeing, too, with what powers the judicious ruler is invested for the rectification of mankind, for re-moulding, re-forming men, we may imagine him asking, like Pilate, whom he shall release unto you?—the Malefactor or the Benefactor?

F

ADDENDA.

Some Considerations touching the Outcry for Technical Education.*

H<small>AD</small> the compilers of Dictionaries lived a few years longer, they would not have accompanied the word *technical* with the comment 'not in common or popular use,' for now it is in everybody's mouth, either willingly or per force, and in a limited sphere technical education has become a 'cry.' But there are few people who use the word in connection with that of education precisely know what they mean. The word *technical*, meaning that which appertains to the arts, is capable of a very wide application ; and a complete technical knowledge would comprise that of the entire arts of life. For many years England had a greater technical knowledge and skill than any other country in Europe, and was, *par excellence*, the workshop of the world ; and technical education in so far as it concerns the workman, is best acquired in the workshop. Other nations were not anything like so completely, or on so large a scale 'workshops,' but of late years there have not been wanting signs to show that foreigners are not quite contented with their fine art, war panoply, and palatial grandeur, but desire to have workshops

* 'Art : Pictorial and Industrial,' December 1871. Charles Burton.

and to become shopkeepers too. What was to be done by the Continentals? England had long been in the market, and her power of work known to the world. Orders were not likely to flow to countries as yet comparatively without either workmen or workshops. England's technical supremacy had been gradually and quietly attained. Therefore to the question, 'What was to be done?' there was but one solution, viz. to institute State Workshops, Technical Schools, and endeavour to raise workmen by an artificial process, a forcing process which very much reminds one of the scheme for hatching by steam—hence the origin of the technical system of the Continent, the *ars et métiers*, &c., &c., which have set the enthusiastic English copyist agog. Your Englishman, that is to say, your upper and middle class Englishman, cannot be made to understand the *raison d'être* of these foreign institutions; and the great danger which now threatens us is lest our educational copyists should allow their zeal and admiration of foreign institutions to outrun a wiser discretion, and so lead to a tampering with, and ultimately to the supplanting of, the *real* workshop, with that poor substitute, the technical institution, which was devised for an altogether different national organisation.

We must leave the workshop alone if we still desire to maintain English pre-eminence in manufacture; it is not there where the lever is required, not in the performance of work, but to raise the status of its scientific direction; to effect this more ample means must be afforded to that middle-class, the inventors, directors, masters, and managers, to become acquainted with theoretical and applied science; but to attain this end does not require very extensive and elaborate means. It is, above all things, important that the middle man should feel that more is required of him, and then the central polytechnic or other college may be of advantage both to himself and the nation.

The wholesale technical education proposed should be regarded too from another point of view. Are we of so cosmopolitan a temper as to desire *technically* to educate the world? Because every feature of our technical schools would be immediately copied in those countries where that form of institution has long been naturalised for the purpose of instructing their workmen in *English* skill. The English manufacturer and workman, however, by no means desire to inform the world so readily, and at their own expense, as our philanthropic *technical* educators so earnestly desire; they are more exclusive and prefer to keep recent improvements as long as possible to themselves. It is well known that our manufacturers very reasonably object to making the Great International Exhibitions technical schools for the whole world. This may, at first sight, appear to be a selfish policy; but they are only striving to effect in a more direct way what our zealous but mistaken enthusiasts of technical education profess to aim at, but would, if they were allowed to have their own way, most certainly prevent, viz., the preservation of our technical superiority as long as possible. Have we not, in all conscience, been liberal enough to the world, only to witness our own inventions everywhere ruthlessly turned against us? And it must be highly gratifying to our mental workers, our brain workers, who devote themselves to the improvement of the industrial arts, to find a scheme proposed for depriving them and the country as early as possible of the fruits of their labour. If, therefore, our technical superiority is to be preserved, we earnestly counsel the workman's mistaken friends to leave him alone to acquire his technical education in that school which has made him so famous, the workshop itself, and even then the outside world will acquire the knowledge of our most recent improvements quite soon enough. If it be wrong to endeavour to keep our advanced knowledge to ourselves, it is equally wrong to desire to main-

tain our manufacturing superiority; the high morality would
be to be pleased to see our neighbours as clever, if not
cleverer than ourselves.

But in truth the thought or instinct of self-preservation
comes in before such lofty considerations. To give up all
our improvements to the world as soon as discovered would
be to commence charity abroad, when everyone knows it
'*should begin at home.*' The English family is far too large
for its heads to be generous before they are just, to forget
the clamorous mouths at home, and inconsiderately scatter
our well-earned advantages broadcast to the nations. New
ideas, inventions, improvements, are property—as much so
as jewels, money, or land; and whoever seeks to deprive a
man of them, or of his rights in them, is a more despicable
thief than the housebreaker, for it is a kind of property which
cannot well be kept under lock and key, and must, in most
cases, be entrusted to men's honour. If you will not protect
the property of your brain-workers, be consistent and pro-
claim Communism at once, for you have far less right to
retain any other property undistributed. The nation never
dreams that it is living on the legacies of a few brain-workers,
such as Watt, Arkwright, Stephenson, &c. That it is to the
foresight and inventive power of two or three men that the
enormous riches of this country and its start in the race of
nations are mainly due, and not, as it is too often foolishly
supposed, to the intellectual shrewdness and superiority of
this generation. Let us beware of laying that flattering
unction to our souls, and in vanity and purse pride, snubbing,
passing over, or killing the genius which would carry on the
torch and maintain the nation's status in the future. Let us
beware in all our fussification and outcry about science
teaching, lest the men who could possibly serve us be lost;
for it should be recollected that the great men we have
referred to were not indebted to any system of technical

education. The men of most use to the country can, as a general rule, educate themselves. It is the men who either cannot or will not educate themselves about whom the State need most concern itself ; but surely we cannot count upon these for the maintenance of the manufacturing supremacy of the country.

The workshop is the best technical college for the workman ; he requires no extraneous science-teaching in handicraft, that is a matter of experience, of the gradual training of the eye and hand upon the work itself. Whereas the meddlesome projector would convert the mechanic into a nondescript, neither master nor workman. What science the artisan desires could be obtained from popular lectures, and by way of hobby or recreation. No scheme of technical education can be devised to meet the subtle gradations in work, and the sweeping plan proposed would only serve to upset the balanced adjustment of technical education as that is now apportioned in various degrees, and would end in producing too many masters without capital and diminishing the number of good workmen. On principle we would say, ' Let every kind of technical education be provided for by voluntary effort, and left to individual selection and acquirement.' The State, in its watchful guardianship, only taking care that the Schools and Colleges of the realm be sufficiently numerous for the requirements of the people. The frightful mischief which may be caused by injudicious meddling may be faintly conceived from a fragment of a Devonshire Farmer's speech on Education, reported in the *Daily News* of Nov. 1. The true policy is, not to teach too much, but only those few essential subjects which form the key to the rest ; leaving much to be acquired, to choice, to individual energy. Then we shall have men's knowledge properly graduated to special purposes, and thorough technical education without any mischievous interference.

The Englishman, when once he gets an idea, like that of technical education, into his head, shuts his eyes, bends to the notion, and goes headlong into confusion—he cannot formulate and adjust. What we now require to determine is,—1, The essential or fundamental education, which should be common to all men ; having determined that, we may proceed to the consideration of—2, the means for *special* education and the necessary institutions for effecting it. But it will be of very little consequence what institutions be founded or organisation adopted if you cannot find a nation in earnest ; if you cannot make your Englishman think that he has something more to do than to trifle his life away, all the science-teaching in the world will only leave his work soulless, slipshod, and blundering.

But it is an illusory supposition that England, let her be as earnest as she may, and provided with every educational advantage, will always preserve the same distance between herself and pursuers ; the quality of work is final—no nation can attain to more than well-designed and thoroughly good work. Foreigners will pass us if we abate in earnestness and speed, but will overtake us if we keep at our best. We cannot reasonably expect for ever to monopolise the work of the world. Continental wars may check the dissipation of that monopoly for a time, but the day must come when we shall have to share it, and for that day we must prepare ourselves. Meanwhile, we must endeavour to relieve the island of its enormous human freight, not however, as some wonderful philanthropists would have it, by sending out only those of good character, or misery and starvation will increase to a frightful extent. No technical education in the world will avert the general diffusion of industry in Europe ; so, whilst conclaves are pondering upon the right thing to do in regard to education, surplus population to the West ! or anywhere where you can find elbow room.

The Education of the Workman.*

AGITATORS have now for several years been disquieting themselves and the British public about the hopeless technical condition of the English workman; but they have been in a great measure unnecessarily disquieting themselves and the public. The English workman has by this time pretty well learnt to take care of himself, and tolerably well knows the kind of education he requires: and whatever strides Continental working men may have recently made, he is still in the aggregate unapproached in technical skill, as M. Taine frankly acknowledges. But it would be well if the general public had clear ideas on the subject of our topic.

Men require, as stated in the preceding article, two kinds of education: 1st. That essential to the development of the manhood; 2dly. The special, or the professional and technical. Of these two kinds, the first, or *Essential*, is the more important, and that about which state and voluntary effort should be the most solicitous. For in respect to educational training, that is men's common need, a need which should be equally supplied to peasant and peer; and which being supplied, we might confidently await results. To this the *Special*, though also important, should be secondary and subordinate, and acquired either in the college, the office, the factory, or workshop.

As we found that Education, so we also find that Work may be broadly divided into two kinds, viz., Brain-work and Hand-work. The first is that of the thinker, of the philosopher, poet, mathematician, physicist; the second that of the artisan, workman, and labourer. But there are men whose work is variously differentiated between these two extremes, and whose business it is to be informed in both science

* 'Art: Pictorial and Industrial,' December 1871. Charles Burton,

and handicraft—who should thoroughly understand work, and be alive to its improvement and economical production by the application of science; these are the men on whom our prolonged manufacturing precedence will mainly depend. There is also the artist who in himself combines the functions of brain and hand-work; and who occupies as it were an exact middle place. Now it is these middle men whose business it is to be informed in science and handicraft, who stand most in need of that *special* education of which we hear so much, called *technical*, the inventor, the painter, the sculptor, the engineer (naval, military, and civil), the mechanician, the architect, the chemist; who require, in fact, more mathematics, more mechanics, more chemistry, more thorough theoretical insight—for whom additional science-teaching, Special Colleges, should be instituted. But it should at the same time be remembered that this *middle rank* is comparatively not a large class to provide for, or the agitation and demand may be out of all proportion to the need. It is precisely the class standing most in need of technical education which is so very anxious to accord it to that which requires it least.

In respect to the education of the workman, it may at the outset be admitted that no appetite for knowledge should be checked unless it tend to interfere with mental digestion, as that universal scientific cramming contemplated most assuredly would, and neither improve the artisan nor his work. What then does the English workman really educationally require? We reply, more of the humanizing formative elements of education—the proper training of the eye and ear, the discipline of his rational faculty—that training, in brief, which would make him morally and physically a man. The workman knows this and is not to be blinded by sophistries with reference to scientific teaching. He full well knows that a sound intellect and physique will enable him to perfectly execute any work by sheer practice in the use of his eye, hand, and tools, guided by the traditional experience of the craft imparted in the factory or workshop. He by no means undervalues science, and knows its province, but it is of no use in that which entirely depends on skill or dexterity of hand. It is not for its utility, but for its own sake that he desires to be acquainted with it—unless he be ambitious of becoming a middle man. Science is with him a recreative study—art, music, literature, and science are as much the complementaries to hand-work as physical exercise to brain-work; be it, however, always remembered that compensating recreations must be lightly touched, never with the energy of those with whom such studies or such exercise are the lifework and real business. It is in default of this knowledge and the prudence which it engenders that health seeking is so often turned to health wreck.

We are in hope that the School Board will devise the proper system for the central or essential form of education. But as adjuncts to this, there should be the reading, art class, singing class, and lecture room scattered broadcast—also more institutions on the pattern of the Working Men's College, in Great Ormond Street; for institutions on that model would afford opportunities to the artisan ambitious and conscious of powers for another field of work, of acquiring that more extensive education which would fit him for it at a very moderate cost: and perhaps a similar organisation to that of the ancient guilds might be turned to account, in seeking out and noting the imperfections in processes, and communicating them for solution and improvement to the scientific authorities at the Polytechnic College.

What we above all things require in this country is the critical faculty of adjustment rather than the pursuit of one educational panacea for all our short-comings. Our educational system will be simplified as the world advances. At present, however, and fortunately, the English workman is free from the deteriorating effect of the cramming system to which the middle class is becoming more and more exposed, and which prevents that robust and independent action which characterises the unsurfeited and untrammelled mind. The workman's intellect at the present time goes more directly to its mark, and the roots of great questions, than the classes supposed to be above him in the social scale—just as it did with the middle classes before their education was marred by too great extension, made wider but shallower, more superficial. The victory is to him who thinks earnestly and deeply, if the reason be rightly ordered, rather than to men crammed with second-hand knowledge, acquainted with and appreciative of those formal niceties upon which the cultivated man prides himself, without having the bark of rougher kind on which to engraft them. So difficult is it to hit the true point between the coarse vigour and effeminacy of the intellect, that mid-point which gives those true forms to intellect and work which constitutes perfection.

------

*Letters on Technical Education and the Trades' Guild of Learning.**

As I have for so many years been an advocate of education, and more especially of the education of the workman, I am not likely to be suspected of any sinister motive in opposing the present project. I have a strong conviction that, notwithstanding the good intentions of the promoters of this scheme, it tends towards a misdirection of energy and confounding of purposes. We do not appear in England to

* 'The Builder,' June 21, 1873.

have a faculty for organising, discriminating, and rightly divid-
ing functions.   It is at one time all physical training, now all
science, then all technical education.   The hog, the whole
hog, and nothing but the hog.   Now the trades' guilds of old
had special functions, and immense advantages would, no
doubt, accrue to all crafts if the ancient and special functions
of these guilds were revived,—viz., that of collecting all
information having reference to the technicalities of their
respective crafts, and providing for their improvement, by the
appointment of fit persons to investigate processes, to communicate the results of these inquiries, and to answer questions submitted to them.   The guilds might also gradually
become tribunals to which disputes between masters and
workmen could be referred.   These functions were allotted
to the guilds in my paper on the Organisation of Education
which appeared some twelve months since in these columns.
The educational function should be entrusted to working
men's colleges, and I proposed in that paper that the Art-
schools of the Science and Art Department should be converted into institutions of that kind.   The functions of general education and technical inquiry and study would then be
distinctly divided, and each would be better attended to and
performed.

Charles Burton clearly pointed out in his articles on
'Technical Education,' which appeared in 'Art, Pictorial
and Industrial,' that technical education and technical institution on an extensive scale were more a necessity of
foreign countries than our own.   For other nations,—to
emulate the industry of England, and being comparatively
without, had to improvise workshops.   England has, and
has had for centuries, the best of all technical colleges,
—her great factories.   He also pointed out in that journal
the mischief that is likely to ensue from an indiscriminate
provision for technical education.   There are degrees and
special functions even in the various crafts, a wholesome

division of duties. The science and mental direction properly belong to the masters. Skill of hand and eye, of handicraft, is another and distinct function, and belongs to the workman. You are hastening, by your misdirected efforts, to confound these separate and distinct vocations, and to increase the causes of bickering between master and man.

Another curious inconsistency appears to me to crop up in the discussions on these matters, viz., the solicitude evinced to confer the advantages of a *university education* on the workman,—the advantages of that education observe ! which has long since been pronounced unsatisfactory, and quite out of harmony with the times. No, sir, the education of the workman must be something quite different to that, not only for his own, but for the country's sake, in which it is predicted, he is to take a more prominent political part. What it should be, I have some time since endeavoured to set forth in a lecture delivered at the Working Men's College, which was, I believe, fully reported in the *Builder*.

July 10, 1873.

I MUST confess that I had somewhat misapprehended the project of the Trades' Guild of Learning when I addressed a letter to the Editor of the *Builder*; but although I misunderstood the title, I had not the wholesale and indiscriminate character of the education which the new institution proposes to offer to the workman. The Guild proposes to do too much to do that much well. We pile institution upon institution and complicate the machinery of educational and other organisations, instead of simplifying and judiciously reconstructing and readjusting the resources at our command. And even before anything can well be attempted in this direction, we must have clear notions upon the subject of education itself. Are we to proffer the old-fashioned education of the universities, which has long since been condemned, to the workman? The education of which the Rev. Sydney Smith said, ' It is vain to say we have produced great men under this system; we have produced great men under all systems. Every Englishman must pass half his life in learning Latin and Greek; and Classical learning is supposed to have produced the talents which it has not been able to extinguish. It is scarcely possible to prevent great men from rising up under any system of education, however bad:' and again, ' If it be urged that public schools have only assumed their present character within the last century, or half-century, and that what are now called public schools partook, before this period, of the nature of private schools, there must be added to our lists the names of Milton, Dryden, Addison, &c., &c., and it will follow that the English have done all that they have done in the Arts and Sciences without the aid of that system of education to which they are now so much attached.' And following in the wake of this liberal writer, we may add, also, that neither were the men who invented and carried out those utilities which have furnished England with such tremendous means of power and wealth, thus educated.

What would they with our workmen? We do not want them to be ' coddled ' and spoilt by schemes for ' forcing ' technical education, but to continue the robust, efficient workmen they have long been; and to preserve this robustness and efficiency, we must above all things be fully impressed with the superiority of *quality* over *quantity* in education.

The great problem to be solved is this : ' What is the Essential or Setting-Up education which should be provided for every man in the State?' The next: ' What can be done to improve the quality of work?' I conscientiously believe that in this case it would be the wisest course to interfere as little as possible. Professional or technical education should be left to private, to trade enterprise, to the *special* college, the office, and the workshop ; in order that some gradation of social distinction may be preserved, and that the technical education may be really practical and beneficial. The State has a right to provide the essential education : that central form of it which puts the keys of knowledge into every man's hands ; but not to unlock every department of knowledge indiscriminately to the whole population. Something should be left to be self-earned, and as marks of talent, industry, and social position. Would you tax the classes above, in order to place the children of those in a different grade on an equal professional or technical educational footing with their own ? If you should, you will not only be unjust, but you will too rapidly break down all social landmarks and produce irretrievable mischief and confusion. All that is really required to set special, *i.e.* technical education in order, is a revival of the Trades' Guilds for this practical purpose ; to increase the number of Working Men's Colleges by the extension or conversion of the Art-Schools of the Science and Art Department already proposed, and the establishment of several Special Colleges.

General taste and refinement would be the inevitable results of making fine art and music, or shall we say drawing and music, two of the essential elements of our system of national education.

I beg to thank you for kindly returning my MS. You know that the Working Men's Club and Institute Union has my cordial sympathy ; and I believe that the organisation of popular lectures will be attended with good results ; for I take the entertainment of the workman to be a most important consideration.

But to explain more precisely what my fears are. Though the Guild of Learning may not be intended to make working men Latin and Greek scholars, let me put the subject in the following form :—

There will presently be—

1. The common education of the School Board Schools, which I fear will embrace too many subjects.

2. The thoroughly scientific or technical education for the masters and directors of work, obtainable in schools and colleges.

3. The practical education of the workman, hand and eye, in the workshop.

4. Lectures for entertainment—Popular Lectures.

Now, the danger lies in the erroneous supposition that the master and workman in any craft require the same kind of *special* education. Theirs are two distinct vocations (2 & 3). Take a working engineer, for instance. A knowledge of science is by no means necessary for him ; he may become a first-rate workman without the slightest scientific knowledge. Good workmanship depends upon accuracy of eye and dexterity of hand, not upon scientific information. Now, if the technical educators, in their *trop de zèle*, give the workman, at a nominal cost, that technical instruction which the masters or directors can only obtain at a great expense, they will not only make the workman and the workman's children the competitors of the masters and the masters' children, but they will make the workman a discontented and worse workman by dissipating instead of concentrating his energy ; and, be it remembered, our technical educators would tax the masters to bring about these results.

Dr. Johnson says, ' There is nothing which we would not

rather know than not, if it were only to be known for the wishing.'   But, in truth, in knowledge, as in everything else human, if we add in one direction it must be by subtracting in another.   We must therefore be content with the power of thinking and working well, without knowing everything.

The duty of the State, I take it, is rather to train men properly, to put them intellectually and physically in the proper condition for the start in life, to give the right educational setting-up, than to cram with knowledge.   The State should of course give that essential knowledge which, though it does not embrace many subjects, is the most important, as being the key to all the rest.   Depend upon it, it is the *quantity* of information now proffered which is working and will continue to work mischief in England.   There cannot be the least doubt that new educational arrangements are required for improving the knowledge of the workman, but it is not in the direction which those who are not intimately and practically acquainted with his requirements would suppose.

The Organisation of Education, Civil, Military, and Naval.*

With the exception of the imperfect provision for the education of the masses, which, we trust, will now soon be remedied, there is, perhaps, no other country in the world which possesses such a wealth of scholastic institutions as Great Britain; but these are so disconnected and deficient in any concerted plan of action, that their power is in a great mea-

* 'The Builder,' April 6, 1872.

sure frittered away, and thus they fail to exercise that larger and healthier influence which would inevitably be consequent on united action.

Being painfully impressed, several years ago, with this terrible absence of organisation in the educational forces already at our disposal, I ventured to address the following letters to the editors of the *Daily News* and the *Builder*. These are given in the order in which they appeared. That to you, October 31st, 1868, was headed,—

THE AFFIX 'MASTER OF ARTS.'—'Felix Summerly' did good service the other day by directing attention, through the medium of the columns of the *Builder*, to the greater consideration and larger share of time devoted to the study of art in the Continental colleges and schools than in England. This opens a question of great moment, a subject requiring thorough ventilation. Is not the affix 'Master of Arts' a delusive sign of a complete education, when it may be, and is commonly, earned by men theoretically and practically unacquainted with the two great arts of painting and music? The classics, it is true, were for many centuries the only studies which kept alive the spirit of art, and therefore gradually assumed a prescriptive and undue importance in the college curriculum, which, in due time, strengthened into an overweening prejudice in their favour difficult to combat. There are, however, signs at the ancient seats of learning of a better temper, and a more gracious bending to the times. The more modern collegiate institutions 'go in' for everything, not only for the classics and the mathematics, but science, chemistry, and medicine,—but even in these there is still small, if any, provision for the two symbols of civilisation,— painting and music. This is strange when it has been so long admitted that an improved taste is daily becoming a more crying national need, for the present and future credit of our manufactures; nevertheless, though such an educational reform promises greater mercantile prosperity, a plethora of wealth, the country remains unmoved, to any sensible extent, even by the prospect of the promised golden reward. This immobility, after the importance of a change has been long demonstrated, is truly English.

When the Schools Commission was pursuing its useful work in 1865, I took advantage of a professional position, to call the attention of one of its body to the disadvantages under which the study of art in our colleges and schools commonly labours, and, whilst urging the importance of the study, and the immediate necessity for some reform in this direction, I stated that the study of art was not merely important as the proper means of educating men to appreciate the beautiful, but in the direct utilitarian point of view,—for that, when drawing is properly taught, it is a most potent means for perfecting the faculty of observing correctly, of looking at things rightly,—of enabling people, in fact, to see properly. How inaccurately people do generally observe what is before, or going on around them, is only fully known to art-teachers and frequenters of the Courts of Justice ; and this will continue till the importance of training the two leading senses of sight and hearing be a thoroughly recognised and important object of education. It is not, therefore, a matter of indifference, I urged, how drawing is taught in public and private schools; whether the students be condemned to *makeshift* in respect to time and place of study ; whether the time set apart for it be pinched in between the more favoured claims of Greek and Latin, or carried on in the class-room, the worst lighted and adapted to the purpose. Moreover, the slight consideration it receives is too frequently aggravated by the so-called 'practice of drawing' being nothing more than mere crude water-colour blotching, and that more than half performed by the teacher. For the study of art to fulfil its true educational function, it should beget a habit of exact comparison, and this is only to be induced by experienced teachers conversant with that thorough discipline and training of the eye which is acquired in the art-school proper,—the student commencing his studies from the simpler forms of leaves, fruit, and flowers, and gradually rising step by step, to grapple with the subtleties of the human form. One great hindrance to the introduction of a better system of studying drawing in schools is doubtless the ignorant satisfaction which parents evince at those wonderful landscape performances, enlivened with impossible rustic figures and dwel-

lings, surrounded with a blaze of impossible foliage. Such performances are unfortunately too often preferred to the dry and
less showy but more useful work under a good teacher.

In returning to the subject of the 'footing' on which art ought to
stand in our great seminaries of learning, I would ask why it should
not be the same as that of the more favoured subjects? Have
there not been already sufficient reasons adduced why it should
be so placed? An art student, too, ought to have it in his power
to pursue his general, simultaneously with his special study, and
to take the degrees of B.A. and M.A. The question then which
naturally suggests itself to me is this,—whether, as the re-
organisation of our educational system must soon become an
important consideration, it would not be better that every college
should adopt a *leading* speciality. Then we should have a College of the Fine Arts, of Medicine, of Engineering, &c., in which
the degrees of B.A. and M.A. could be graduated for as well as
the special honours of R.A., M.D., or C.E. The plan would have
this advantage, that the greatest talent in each speciality could
be concentrated. This would appear to me to be the best mode of
combining special with general studies, and one which would
not materially disturb our present educational prejudices.
Oxford might retain the classics as its speciality, Cambridge the
mathematics. The Royal Academy or South Kensington might
be transformed into a College of the Fine Arts, the College of
Physicians into a great Medical College, and so on.

We will now turn to the letter addressed to the editor of
the *Daily News*, December 28th, 1868. This had more immediate reference to the Slade Professorship; but it
incidently touches upon the more general question of the
organisation of education :—

Although I have from time to time advocated the establishment of a Faculty of Fine Arts in each of the principal universities, I have only recently become aware of the existence of the
Slade bequest for that purpose, and I think you will agree with
me that for the interests of art it would be well if the
chief features of this codicil were made more widely known.
There is no less a sum than £45,000 bequeathed, free from

legacy-duty, by the late Felix Slade, of Walcot-place, Lambeth, to endow, within two years after his decease, three or more professorships in the universities of Oxford and Cambridge, and also in University College, London ; moreover, to endow six exhibitions or scholarships for proficiency in fine arts, for students under nineteen years of age. And if, after providing for these several trusts and purposes, there shall be any surplus, it shall be applied for the encouragement, benefit, and advancement of the fine arts in England, and every part of such surplus which shall not be so applied within five years is to fall to the residuary personal estate. I have recently proposed that every college should have a leading speciality, so that a student in any of the liberal arts would be able to matriculate at the same time, and under one roof, for his general and special degrees. There would be, according to this proposal, the College of Fine Arts, the College of Medicine, the College of Engineering, &c. A student would not then have to run hither and thither to pick up an education under difficulties. This proposal, however, is but a compromise, or rather one collateral to that for a Grand Central College, submitted to the Royal Commission in 1851, and which provided that all the means for a general and special education should be concentrated in one locality. A proposal to convert the Royal Academy into a College of Fine Arts would at first sight appear to be an impracticable one, and indeed may be so now ; but had the Slade bequest been available before the new buildings at Burlington House were commenced, the Royal Academy might have been justified in considering whether it should not separate its schools from its exhibitions, and carry them on under the roof of University College—whether it could not combine its own with the resources of the bequest. At the College there would be every facility for studying anatomy, chemistry, &c., on the spot. As this conjuncture, however, did not occur, University College cannot hope to make art its dominant speciality ; it would be useless to attempt a ' little ' rivalry with the Royal Academy and South Kensington. The only course, then, which appears to be left open to the council of the college, is to proportion its intended art department to its place in a comprehensive scheme of general education ; and a very important position, I conceive, that should be.

So far back as 1865, whilst the Schools Commission was pursuing its useful course, I took occasion to direct the Commissioners' attention to the fact that the study of art was not only important to educate men to appreciate the beautiful, but to train them to observe, to see correctly what is passing before them. How imperfectly,—inaccurately,—people do observe, is only fully known to art-teachers and Queen's counsel. Some painters may think that the establishment of the faculty proposed would only tend to swell the numbers of an already overcrowded pursuit; but it should be borne in mind that the college art-classes would at the same time cultivate a taste for and an appreciation of art in students never intending to follow art as a profession. We must reach that point, too, as in countries where art is more widely cultivated than in our own, when the fact must be recognised that all who study art cannot be painters, sculptors, and architects, but that some students must direct their talents to the manufactures. The whole question, however, requires careful consideration before it is perceived how important are the benefits to be derived from a more extended study of art.

But long before writing these letters, and so far back as 1850, I had projected the foundation of a Grand Central College of Art, Literature, and Science, at South Kensington or elsewhere, already referred to, and that the surplus fund of the first International Exhibition should be devoted to the realisation of the project. In projecting this central college, the ruling idea which possessed my mind was this,—that the central college should be the institution to which all other educational establishments in the kingdom should converge, and that every means should be used to enlist the best representatives of every department of inquiry, in either hemisphere, as its professors; and thus to make London the great educational centre of the world. All other scholastic institutions were, according to my conception, to graduate up to this. The pamphlet which contained this first suggestion for a Central Polytechnic College was in the hands of the Royal Commissioners of the Exhibition of 1851.

We are all, I believe, now coming to understand the first
and foremost condition of a true system of education, viz.,
the importance of deciding those subjects which are essential to the development of the manhood,—that knowledge
and training which give a man the power of turning himself
to good account in whatever *speciality* he may select ; which
complete him mentally and physically as a man.   These
subjects are very many fewer than most people are apt to suppose,—and should form the real nucleus of every educational
course in the kingdom.   There is no practice which requires
more repeated condemnation than that of 'cramming' too
many subjects into the curriculum of general education.   I
believe that both mental and physical power are weakened
by an ignorant persistence in this course; that practical
capacity is lowered rather than raised by the too-prevalent
educational fashion.

National education, then, may be broadly divided into two
important and distinct sections : first that central or general education which should be accorded to *all* ; and, secondly,
that special or professional education which should be provided for *some* ; and as most men in England are destined
for some special work, the organisation of the special or professional section of education becomes a very important
subject for consideration.

The nation has of late years got a notion that special or
technical education is a very important thing, and has some
bearing upon national interests.   The country has tortured
itself into the utmost confusion on the subject, and is now
intent on providing and applying remedies precisely where
they are not wanted.   Let us consider for a moment that
there are two estates of the realm which require this professional, special, or technical education,—viz., the middle and
the working classes.   Now, for the technical education of
the latter, or the working class, there is no country on the

whole earth in which this kind of education is so well provided for. The college in which the English workman obtains his special education is, as Charles Burton well observes, 'the workshop,' * and the workshops in England are unsurpassed. Yet it is precisely in this direction that the public is clamouring for technical education. 'It is not here,' as the writer just named rightly observes, 'that technical education is required,' and with the caution, 'beware how you interfere with the workshop!' It is the special or professional education of the middle and wealthier classes which urgently needs improvement. The office cannot do for the articled pupil what the shop can do for the apprentice. The professional pupil requires, before or after passing through the office, a wider range of study touching upon his *speciality* than could by any possibility be acquired there. All the professions, therefore, require their own special colleges, as I have previously suggested. This need has recently been felt by some of the professions, and the system has received further extension in proposals for two more special colleges, 'the Legal' and 'the Naval.' The mention of the latter leads me to note that the military and naval education of the country ought to be a part of a comprehensive educational scheme. The following list of special colleges exhibits the extension of the principle in conformity with my own views :—

Theological, Civil Service (Diplomatic, Social Science, &c.) ; Fine Arts, Music, Mathematical (Astronomy, Physics, &c.) ; †Legal, Military, †Naval, Medical, †Engineering, Chemical, Mineralogical, †Zoological (Veterinary, &c.) ; †Agricultural, †Preceptors, Ancient Literature, Modern ditto, Pharmaceutical, Mercantile (Colonial, &c.), Oriental.

---

* 'Art : Pictorial and Industrial.'
† Special colleges already existing, or about to be established.

The centre of this system of *special* colleges would be the Grand Central Polytechnic College already referred to : which if carried out on the scale proposed by me in 1851, would bring all the special colleges under one roof ; in that case the special education, of London professionals, would be provided for in one locality. Such an institution, however, might prove too colossal for convenient management, so that I think the central institution should represent the head of the system of special colleges, and that the highest representative of each of the specialities tabulated should occupy a chair in the Central Institution, from which he would have to lecture on his particular subject, at stated times, to any students of the special colleges then assembled. This Central Institution should also have libraries and museums on an extensive scale, and be the centre from which all London diplomas should be dated. Under this arrangement the special colleges for London would exist as separate institutions, conveniently located, and ranged at moderate distances around the central college.

The several kinds of institution necessary for the educational welfare of the country appear to me to be the following :—

The Central College, Special Colleges, Public Schools for the youth of both sexes (established for several degrees of citizens, and to meet difference of means) ; Private Schools, District Military Schools, ditto Naval ditto, Volunteer Officers' ditto, Working Men's Colleges, School Board Schools.

A more equable distribution of collegiate institutions about the kingdom is also very much needed. It is a very great inconvenience and expense to provincials to have to send up and support young men at any one of our few educational centres, and a practice which is not unfrequently fraught with mischief. Every county town of importance ought to have its properly-constituted medical college, where young men intended for that profession might matriculate *pari passu* for their special and general degrees. I very much doubt whether medical schools ought to be attached to hospitals ; it would, it appears to me, be a better plan to have properly-located medical colleges, the students being permitted to 'walk the hospitals' lying in their own particular district.

The Royal Academy should either be a college of art, or simply a syndicate to confer degrees and appoint the most able masters of the theories of painting, sculpture, and architecture to the art-professorships at the central college. The special college of the fine arts, the schools, and annual exhibitions could then be transferred to other management.

All colleges but the central, let me repeat, should have but one leading subject,—one *speciality*. The misfortune at present appears to me to be this, that every college is trying to make itself as comprehensive as we propose the *central* institution should be, without having the means, the money, or the room to carry out the ambition of its directory ; and, therefore, the attempt only complicates, encumbers, and involves the management.

With respect to the establishment of public schools, I would merely suggest that such should be instituted on a similar plan to those of which the middle class can avail itself, but on a reduced scale of fees, in order to meet the more limited means of the lower middle and upper working classes.

There are two other institutions on my list about which I have something to say, viz.—District Military Schools and Working Men's Colleges. And, first, of the Military Schools,— which will probably form the basis of the localisation of our military forces.

Every district should have its military school, graduated to the requirements of youths training for commissioned officers, non-commissioned officers, and privates. There should be drill-grounds and workshops for instructing the boys, destined for private soldiers, in employments which would render the army, as much as possible, independent of any non-military artificers. These Military Schools would be special, professional, or technical schools—the workshop in which the soldier would be made. The establishment of these schools, and the localisation proposed, would, I firmly believe, render the voluntary military system adequate to all our requirements. Naval Schools, on a similar plan, should be established on the seaboard.

And now, touching the institution called the Working Men's College. I have no doubt in my own mind that that in Great Ormond Street is destined to be the precursor— has been, indeed, already—of many similar institutions throughout the kingdom. Colleges of this kind would fulfil several important and useful functions. They would afford opportunities to workmen and others, having but limited means, to improve and extend their information in their leisure hours. In Ormond Street there are classes for the study of Greek, Latin, history, art, mathematics, physiology, &c., at a very small term-fee. The programme is as extensive as that of the great universities ; but it can seldom fall to the lot of working men to be able to take advantage of the entire course : yet it always affords men the opportunity of taking one or two subjects in which they may be specially interested ; and now and then, when a man is conscious of possessing superior ability, to educate himself up to the higher mark he has proposed. But that this kind of institution may be of an extended national advantage, I think they must become a part of the Government scheme of education. It can scarcely be expected that any institutions could, as the Ormond Street College, be taught on the voluntary principle, by unremunerated teachers. We have there been bound together by enthusiasm in the cause, and a sincere respect and regard for the Rev. the Principal. It requires great determination, and a rigorously-ordered working life, to be able to give, through the years, regular attendance to duties of this kind. I am therefore inclined to believe that when the merits of this institution, and the useful functions which such colleges are calculated to fulfil, come to be better understood, and the establishment of working men's colleges throughout the great towns be contemplated, the voluntary system of teaching will have, if not entirely, to be partially abandoned. The Rev. the Principal was, however, sanguine that it would not. My own notion is that the most feasible and practicable plan for their extension would be by widening the local and provincial art schools of the Science and Art Department to the functions of working men's colleges.

Finally, I should desire to direct attention to the importance of drawing and music in general education,—in that education which is to form the manhood; they are essentially human and humane studies. The study of the arts would cover those dry bones of physical science, to which modern notions in their cold mechanical pride would confine education. The arts are the golden links in education; they are, too, as utilitarian as those studies to which this virtue is most attributed. I have repeatedly touched upon this subject, and will only now recapitulate the strong arguments in favour of their becoming an essential part of general education, of all college and school courses. Drawing and music are the proper exercises of the two most important of our senses, the eye and the ear. We should bear in mind that it is through the senses of seeing and hearing that we chiefly bear witness to what is passing in the world, and those who have the training of these senses only fully know what false witnesses the senses generally are, before they are properly educated. Neither let it be forgotten that it is upon these generally untrained and neglected senses, that character and life are frequently at stake. The desire to obey the command, 'Thou shalt not bear false witness,' may sometimes be strengthened by being put upon oath, but the truth of evidence cannot be guaranteed by that course. If a witness be an imperfect observer, as the majority of witnesses of course are, in default of proper training, he may, and often does, conscientiously swear to the absolute truth of his erroneous impressions, and he cannot conscientiously do otherwise. In teaching drawing, this moral may be inculcated: 'If you misapprehend the truth with regard to the fact, the model immediately before you, and biding your time for deliberate inspection, how can you expect to correctly observe and accurately record the fleeting facts and occurrences of every-day life?' It is not, however, in the witness-box only that trained senses are required, but to appreciate harmony and beauty in nature, to preside watchfully over all kinds of work, and to endow a nation's manufactures with that taste and permanent excellence which will ensure their appreciation throughout the civilised world. I am now speaking more immediately of the education of the eye, and I will venture to say that you would find that painters and sculptors could more readily be inducted to any kind of handicraft—could more readily turn their hands to any kind of work,—than any other class of the community; and why? Not only because these arts require the greatest dexterity of hand, but because painters and sculptors see better. I know that there is as much to be said in behalf of music as an *essential* study, and has been said by musicians who are more competent than I to speak upon that subject.

The thorough organisation of education should be the question of paramount importance with a nation's rulers. It is education which moulds a people for good or evil. Take care of that, and England may rest hopeful and confident in her future. No difficulties should be permitted to stand in the way, nor expense be spared in order to have it the most complete in the world.

LONDON: PRINTED BY
SPOTTISWOODE AND CO., NEW-STREET SQUARE
AND PARLIAMENT STREET